Oxfam
VEGETARIAN
COOKBOOK

Oxfam
VEGETARIAN
COOKBOOK

Compiled by

Rose Elliot

VERMILION
LONDON

First Published in 1992 by Vermilion
an imprint of Ebury Press
Random House UK Ltd
20 Vauxhall Bridge Road
London SW1V 2SA

Editor: Janet Illsley
Design: Clive Dorman

Oxfam Project Co-ordinator: Robert Cornford
Oxfam Project Administrator: Lucy Whitehurst

Jacket Photography: Michelle Garrett
Food Stylist: Meg Jansz

Food Photography: Martin Brigdale
Stylist: Andrea Lambton
Food Stylist: Judy Bugg

Cataloguing in Publication Data is available from the British Library.

ISBN 0 09175437 2

Typeset by Clive Dorman & Co
Printed and bound in Great Britain

Contents

About Oxfam   6

Introduction   12

Soups   15

Snacks & Starters   27

Salads   37

Vegetable Accompaniments   49

Pasta Dishes   61

Rice & Grain Dishes   73

Bean & Lentil Dishes   85

Savoury Pastry Dishes   95

Main Vegetable Dishes   107

Nut Dishes   127

Puddings   141

Breads, Biscuits & Cakes   159

Preserves & Drinks   177

Index   186

About Oxfam

This book is a project that reflects so much of Oxfam. It links different countries of the world; it combines the enthusiasms of Oxfam volunteers and staff with the welcome support and endorsement of celebrities; it is a celebration of some of the most basic needs of people, for food and companionship. It is also, like Oxfam, profoundly practical. It takes natural ingredients and, through the alchemy of care, advice and preparation, turns them into a range of delicious, tempting and healthy dishes. The recipes have come from many sources: current volunteers in the UK and Ireland; field staff overseas; earlier collections from Oxfam back to *Chefs Galore* published in 1964; Oxfam Canada's volunteers and staff; Oxfam America; Community Aid Abroad's volunteers and staff; celebrities in the UK; and Rose Elliot.

Oxfam is particularly pleased that Rose is associated with this book. She is a long-time Oxfam supporter, wrote a book on vegetable cookery for Oxfam Publications, did demonstrations at Oxfam conferences and until recently had a nephew working for Oxfam in the Middle East.

We hope that Oxfam will be able to talk to a new constituency through this book, and that many readers will make a long-term engagement with Oxfam through its recipes. The addresses of Oxfam offices around the world are at the end of 'About Oxfam': do contact us.

Working for a fairer world

In an age when space travel, the most potent symbol of technological progress, is commonplace you might think that poverty on earth is a thing of the past. You would be wrong.

Every day, millions of people in the countries of the South go without things we in the developed countries of the North take for granted: food, shelter, water, education, health care, and the right to make decisions about our lives.

In fact, for many poor people things are getting worse, not better.

OXFAM is helping people break out of their poverty by supporting them in their efforts to make changes that will last.

OXFAM has been doing this in different ways around the world since 1942.

The early years

In 1942 the world is at war. Most of Europe is occupied by Nazi forces, and innocent civilians are suffering. In Oxford, on 5 October 1942, a group of people form the Oxford Committee for Famine Relief. Its aim: to relieve the suffering of

civilians in Greece where women and children are starving, and to press for supplies to be allowed through the Allied blockade. The Oxford Committee joins with Famine Relief Committees around the country to lobby British and Allied governments. It is partly successful, and a trickle of food is allowed into Greece before the war ends. But it is only after the liberation of Greece in 1944 that the blockade is finally lifted and the trickle becomes a more adequate supply.

The Oxford Committee raises funds and supplies for the Greek Red Cross to support the victims of conflict. Donations come in through appeals to the public, and through a temporary 'gift shop' where the goods are later sold (the forerunner of the now very familiar OXFAM shop).

When peace finally comes the Oxford Committee finds there is still work to do. More than 30 million refugees are moving across the borders of Europe – with no possessions, homes or future. The Oxford Committee continues to raise money and collect clothing for them. The money pays for food and shelter, and the clothing is shipped to frightened and shattered families in Europe, including the recent enemy – Germany.

In June 1948 the first permanent OXFAM shop (a Gift Shop and Collecting Centre) opens in Broad Street, Oxford. There is still one on the site.

The original Oxford Committee doesn't disband. It continues to organise relief for refugees from conflict and for victims of natural disasters. In 1965 the telegram name OXFAM is adopted as the registered name of the charity. It expands its activities and its vision and continues on the road to becoming the OXFAM we know today.

Changing times: OXFAM overseas

OXFAM, which started life helping civilian victims and refugees in war-torn Europe, now works in 77 countries and supports over 2,800 long-term development projects. Much of its work is still in areas where conflict makes life almost unsupportable for its innocent victims. A common thread in OXFAM's development is the commitment to humanitarian help for people, irrespective of religious or political boundaries.

OXFAM started as a famine relief organisation and is still involved in emergency relief following disasters such as drought, flood or war. But OXFAM is also committed to the wider and more lasting relief of suffering. It works alongside the very poorest people developing ways to break free of sickness, illiteracy, powerlessness and poverty, and arguing against the injustice that causes them.

OXFAM helps to challenge the exploitation and injustice that keeps people poor. Local OXFAM staff based around the world keep in regular contact with project partners, giving support and advice and ensuring that grants are well

spent. Many self-help projects are small scale and only need minimal financial support. About a third of the grants OXFAM makes are for under £3,000, but the impact of these small sums is considerable. After decades of experience OXFAM knows that the projects most likely to succeed are those which engage people in working for their own development.

OXFAM's most public face is its response to disasters and emergencies. The OXFAM Emergencies Warehouse is a common image on television with supplies being loaded, often under floodlights, for dispatch to a disaster area. In its early years OXFAM provided shelter, blankets and warm clothes to people displaced by disasters. Now it has a world-wide emergencies service providing water purification, sanitation, medical, housing and other support services as well as funds for materials and skills available at the site of the disaster. Technology has changed over time but the dedication and commitment is the same.

Here are brief accounts of just three projects that OXFAM has supported. They show the very wide range of its work and interests, and – for readers of the *Oxfam Vegetarian Cookbook* – focus on projects associated with food.

In the Kim district of southern **Chad,** rice was grown for six months of the year in fields irrigated from the Logone river. For the other six months there wasn't enough water to irrigate them. The fields lay dry and unused, until women from six villages came together to grow vegetables on the 'dry' land. The women had to keep the crops weeded, and provide irrigation. By the end of the first season they were harvesting tomatoes, lettuce, carrots and onions for their own families, and selling the surplus in local markets. The men of the villages were so impressed by the women's farming skills that they now help out on the vegetable plots. And the success of the plots shows a way of adapting local farming to a drier, more difficult climate.

OXFAM has provided funds to establish the group, to support its marketing effort, and for pest control training.

In the mountainous region of Hoang Lien Son in northern **Vietnam,** farmers grow rice, maize and vegetables on steeply terraced hillsides. In Sa Pa district this traditional growing was threatened as an irrigation canal and weir had fallen into disrepair, and the natural water sources have diminished as a result of deforestation on the hills. The people of Sa Pa are redesigning the canal, and siting a new weir to ensure a continuous supply to the terraces as the water levels fall. This project will both ensure the continued use of existing terraces, and will bring a further 50 hectares of land into productive use. The district's food production will be that much more secure in years to come.

OXFAM has provided construction materials and equipment, and paid for a consignment of rice used to pay local people working on the scheme.

In the **UK,** in partnership with Traidcraft, Twin Trading and Equal Exchange, OXFAM is introducing *Cafédirect,* a new 'fair trade' coffee. *Cafédirect* is a blend

of Latin American and Caribbean beans, launched with supplies from growers in Mexico, Costa Rica and Peru. The beans are grown in mountainous areas, an environment producing the finest arabica beans with a smooth taste.

In **Mexico** the producers are mainly indigenous peoples with small family farms, members of CESCAFE, a co-operative in Chiapas State. In **Costa Rica** the small producers are all members of COOCAFE, a regional association of co-operatives in Guanacaste State. In **Peru,** the 12 small co-operatives in the north east have formed CECOOAG to represent themselves and operate a central export unit.

The small scale of production in these co-operatives reduces the need for chemical inputs in the plantations. The *Cafédirect* order for beans is pre-paid – so the growers do not have to get into debt to finance their crop. By consolidating orders the cost of transport, shipping, roasting and packing is reduced, allowing a higher share of the selling price to be paid direct to the producing co-operatives. And, with long term commitments for their beans, growers can invest in improving their crops. It takes at least four years for a coffee bush to mature – so growers need to know that there is a market for their crop in the future.

Changing times: OXFAM in the UK and Ireland

In 1942 the Oxford Committee was involved in public advocacy – through lobbying, letter writing and public education in its campaign to get aid to Greece through the blockade. Since then campaigning and education has been an integral part of OXFAM's work, informing people and governments in the rich world about what can be done to help poorer people in the countries of the South tackle poverty and global injustice. The *Oxfam Vegetarian Cookbook* is a part of this programme.

OXFAM pioneered the charity shop and for many the term 'OXFAM Shop' *means* charity shop. There are now over 850 OXFAM shops in the United Kingdom and Ireland. You may have bought this book in one.

The OXFAM catalogue has become a regular source of imaginative gifts with over 2.5 million copies distributed each year. The catalogue is crammed with craft goods from groups supported by OXFAM's Bridge programme. Bridge provides an outlet for goods produced as part of self-help development projects, backed up by marketing and training support. Other OXFAMs have developed the Bridge concept: there are similar projects and mail-order catalogues in the USA, Canada, Australia and Belgium.

OXFAM pioneered fund-raising methods that are now commonplace: sponsored walks and rides; pledged giving; concerts (its 21st birthday rally and concert in 1963 was the first of its kind); charity Christmas cards; covenants;

books (OXFAM receives a royalty from every copy of this book sold); national bring-and-buy sales; and many others. Over 60% of OXFAM's funds in the UK and Ireland come from people making donations or a covenanted gift, buying Bridge goods from the catalogue, sending OXFAM cards at Christmas, using OXFAM shops, and taking part in local and national fund-raising events. 79% of the money raised is spent on overseas work and related campaigning and education.

Since 1942 OXFAM has spread across the world, to the USA, to Canada and Quebec, to Australia (where it is called Community Aid Abroad), to Hong Kong, and to Belgium. What started in Oxford is now an international family of independent agencies.

OXFAM: Working for a fairer world

Since 1942 OXFAM's support has been given irrespective of race, colour, gender, politics or religion. This support can come in many ways. It may be:
* an improvement in life for the woman who can draw water from a well in her village without having to walk many kilometres.
* providing shelter and support for the refugee, even for a short time.
* two meals a day, instead of one, as a result of improved agricultural methods.
* a landless farmer finally getting title to some land, and with it the freedom to feed his family.
* the relief given by someone who is prepared to listen to your troubles.
* the joy of a mother whose child's life has been saved by oral rehydration.
* the lifting of some oppression through the activity of an unknown friend in a far country, who cared enough to lobby their MP.

OXFAM gives an opportunity for everyone to make this support possible, to make our world a fairer place.

Here are some ways you can help OXFAM work for a fairer world. You could:
* give good quality books, toys, clothes or other things you no longer need to an OXFAM shop.
* save stamps or coins for OXFAM (drop them off at an OXFAM shop).
* organise a social event (coffee morning, jumble sale or bring-and-buy sale) to raise money for OXFAM.
* talk to other people – your friends, your colleagues, the rest of your family – about ways of working for a fairer world, and get yourself and them involved.
* volunteer your time and your skills to work with OXFAM in a shop, as a campaigner, as a speaker, as a house-to-house collector, as a fund-raiser.
* support 'fair trade' goods whenever they are on sale.
* refuse to give up on the world!

To find out more about OXFAM write to us:

IN ENGLAND:
OXFAM, Anniversary Information, 274 Banbury Road, Oxford OX2 7DZ

IN IRELAND:
OXFAM, 202 Lower Rathmines Road, Dublin 6

IN NORTHERN IRELAND:
OXFAM, PO Box 70, 52-54 Dublin Road, Belfast, BT2 7HN

IN SCOTLAND:
OXFAM, Fleming House, 5th Floor, 134 Renfrew Street, Glasgow G3 3T

IN WALES:
OXFAM, 46-48 Station Road, Llanishen, Cardiff CF4 5LU

IN AUSTRALIA:
Community Aid Abroad, 156 George Street, Fitzroy, Victoria 3065

IN BELGIUM:
OXFAM Belgique, 39 Rue du Conseil, 1050 Bruxelles

IN CANADA:
OXFAM Canada, 251 Laurier Avenue W, Room 301, Ottawa, Ontario KlP 5J6

IN HONG KONG:
OXFAM, Ground Floor - 3B, June Garden, 28 Tung Chau Street, Tai Kok Tsui, Kowloon, Hong Kong

IN NEW ZEALAND:
OXFAM New Zealand, Room 101 La Gonda House, 203 Karangahape Road, Auckland 1

IN QUEBEC:
OXFAM Quebec, 169 Rue St. Paul est, Montreal 127, Quebec H2Y lG8

IN THE USA:
OXFAM America, 115 Broadway, Boston, Massachusetts 02116

Thank you for buying the *Oxfam Vegetarian Cookbook.*

You have already contributed to OXFAM's work as money from each copy sold supports OXFAM's literacy fund.

We hope you will enjoy the book now you know something more about OXFAM and that we can count on your support in the future

WORKING FOR A FAIRER WORLD.

Introduction

I felt honoured when Oxfam invited me to compile a book of vegetarian recipes to celebrate, and raise funds for, their 50th anniversary. The response from friends of Oxfam, whether celebrities or volunteer workers, has been warm and enthusiastic, making this a most happy project on which to work. In requesting contributions to this book, all that we asked was that they should be favourite recipes, and vegetarian. We were delighted at the variety of recipes we received, ranging from soups, starters and salads, to main courses both simple and more elaborate, puddings, cakes and even some pickles and drinks. So, thank you, everyone who responded so generously and enabled us to make this book.

Like Oxfam, vegetarianism and the art of vegetarian cookery have come a long way since 1942. Then, with the country at war, vegetarian recipes were as frugal as any, but they made good use of bread, vegetables, pulses and small quantities of dairy produce in main courses such as lentil savoury, butterbean cutlets and cheese pudding. Advice on cooking vegetables, given in *The Vegetarian News,* October to December 1942 admirably advocates quick cooking in the minimum of water. The emphasis at that time was as much on conserving vitamins as flavour.

Vegetarian cookery reached a new public in 1961 with the opening of Cranks vegetarian restaurants, proving that vegetarianism had in fact progressed beyond the realm of crankiness, although it still had a brown and wholesome image. Chinese and Indian restaurants were also becoming more popular and widespread, offering adventurous vegetarians the chance to try other types of meatless meals. This trend accelerated during the 1970's and 80's, with the introduction of restaurants serving food from countries where tasty vegetarian dishes were part of the normal daily food, not something considered strange and of interest only to food-faddists. And the growing trend towards foreign travel meant that many of us were able to try these dishes in the countries of their origin and pick up numerous other delicious vegetarian ideas too.

I remember what a revelation it was to me, used to being considered a bit of a culinary outcast because of my refusal to eat meat or fish, to realise that most countries of the world had a rich tradition of vegetarian cookery which they took for granted, and on which most of the people lived. Glorious dishes from Italy, France, the Middle East, South America and the Caribbean, India and China, with as much flavour, variety and colour as anyone could wish for.

The influx of ethnic food and ideas, together with the availability of an ever-increasing range of ingredients, and the endorsement of the healthiness of vegetarian food by one research group after another, including the World Health Organisation, brought new interest to vegetarian cookery. Brown gave way to an explosion of bright colours and exciting flavours, heaviness to lightness with the

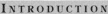
greater use of vegetables, oils, new dairy products, grains, numerous types of pasta, filo pastry... changes which are reflected in many of the recipes in this book, along with some of the best of the old standbys which have become favourites over the years.

We do hope that you will enjoy them all. By buying this book you have already helped Oxfam with its valuable work. By using the recipes to cut down or eliminate meat from your diet and increase the amount of vegetables you eat, you will both improve your health and also help the world's ecology. It takes about 16 kg of vegetable protein to make 1 kg of meat; 80 per cent of the crops grown in Britain and the US are fed to animals, and we still have to import animal feed from the Third World to fatten animals for meat in the West. Huge areas of rainforest are still being destroyed each year to provide grazing land for cattle ranching, when much of the meat is exported to feed the lifestyle of the rich countries of the north. In a world where pure water is becoming a more and more precious and rare commodity it is interesting to note that it takes three times as much water to produce food for a meat-eater as for a vegetarian, twelve times as much as for a vegan.

A major shift in this country towards vegetarianism could have far-reaching effects. The pressure on our farmland would be considerably relieved. More land would be available for natural habitats, and it might also encourage growers to produce food organically. If the use of organically grown produce became widespread in this country it would also be easier for the producers in the Third World to compete with our farmers and sell us their produce. Growing food organically is feasible in many of the countries of the south: it does not involve importing expensive chemical fertilizers or weedkillers from the industrialised countries and, because it is labour-intensive, it provides much-needed employment on the land. At present, however, it cannot compete with the lower prices of our own intensively-grown and subsidised produce. But if everyone was using organic methods, there could be trading on an equal basis. We in the Developed World would benefit as our rivers and streams would become freer of nitrates and chemicals from agricultural run-off. And people eating such a diet would be healthier, with subsequent savings each year on health care...

These things *can* happen. It is up to us, as individuals, in our shopping and cooking habits, to make them happen.

Wishing you good cooking, good eating and good health.

Rose Elliot

Recipe Notes

Quantities are given in metric and imperial measures. Follow one
set of measurements only, not a combination, because they
are not interchangeable.

All spoon measures are level.

Fresh herbs are used unless otherwise stated.

Soups

Asparagus Soup

Serves 4-6

This soup is delicious served either hot or cold.

25 g (1 oz) butter
1 onion, chopped
450 g (1 lb) potatoes, peeled and diced
225 g (8 oz) asparagus
1.75 litres (3 pints) light vegetable stock or water
60 ml (4 tbsp) double cream
dash of lemon juice
salt and freshly ground black pepper

Heat the butter in a large saucepan, add the onion and fry for 5 minutes, until beginning to soften but not brown. Add the potatoes and cook, covered, for a further 5 minutes. Cut off the tough part of the asparagus stems and chop these, then add to the pan. Stir well, then pour in the light vegetable stock or water. Bring to the boil, then cover and simmer for about 20 minutes, until the vegetables are tender. Allow to cool slightly, then purée the mixture in a blender or food processor. Pour through a sieve, back into the saucepan.

While the soup is gently reheating, cut the remaining asparagus into 2.5 cm (1 inch) lengths and cook in a little boiling water for 2-3 minutes, until just tender. Drain and rinse under cold water, to preserve their colour.

Stir the cream into the soup and add a little more water, if necessary, to give a nice light consistency. Add a dash of lemon juice and salt and pepper to taste. Add the rest of the asparagus and reheat gently, or chill, before serving.

ROSE ELLIOT

Lentil and Tomato Soup

Serves 4

*Very popular with my daughter, Claire, this is a cheap, easy and nutritious soup. Serve
it with hunks of bread and some freshly grated cheese.*

30 ml (2 tbsp) olive oil
1 onion, chopped
2 celery sticks, diced
2 carrots, diced
1 garlic clove, crushed
175 g (6 oz) split red lentils
425 g (15 oz) can tomatoes
1 litre (1¾ pints) water
salt and freshly ground black pepper
freshly grated nutmeg

TO GARNISH:
chopped basil

Heat the oil in a large saucepan. Add the onion, cover and cook for 5 minutes,
without browning. Add the celery, carrots and garlic, stir, then cover and cook
for a further 5-10 minutes.

Stir in the lentils, then add the tomatoes, together with their juice, and the
water. Bring to the boil, then simmer for 20-30 minutes, or until the lentils and
vegetables are tender. Add salt, pepper and nutmeg to taste. Sprinkle with
chopped basil before serving.

ROSE ELLIOT

Midweek Soup

Serves 6

An inexpensive meal-in-one soup, which is ideal as a nourishing winter lunch or supper. It is best served with garlic bread or croûtons.

125 g (4 oz) lentils, soaked overnight
125 g (4 oz) marrowfat peas, soaked overnight
450 g (1 lb) onions
450 g (1 lb) carrots
450 g (1 lb) leeks
450 g (1 lb) potatoes, peeled
450 g (1 lb) swede
225 g (8 oz) celery
900 ml (1½ pints) boiling water
1 vegetable stock cube
salt and freshly ground black pepper

Drain the lentils and marrowfat peas and place in a large saucepan. Trim and prepare all of the vegetables as necessary, then dice. Add the vegetables to the saucepan with the water and bring to the boil. Lower the heat, cover and simmer for 45 minutes. Crumble in the stock cube and simmer for a further 10 minutes. Adjust the seasoning and serve with garlic bread, croûtons or crusty wholemeal bread.

CAROL ANN HODGSON • CHESTER-LE-STREET, DURHAM

Peanut Soup

Serves 4-6

This is adapted from a soup which is popular throughout North Sudan, where it is eaten with Kisra – a thin unleavened bread, which is rather like pitta bread. I like to serve my version with pitta bread and a salad – as a lunch or supper.

30 ml (2 tbsp) groundnut or sunflower oil
5 ml (1 tsp) ground coriander
2.5 ml (½ tsp) ground cumin
2 onions, finely chopped
120 ml (8 tbsp) peanut butter
50 g (2 oz) flour
1.2 litres (2 pints) vegetable stock or water
salt and freshly ground black pepper

Heat the oil in a pan and stir in the spices. Add the onions, stir to coat in the spices then lower the heat and cook until the onion is softened. Stir in the peanut butter and flour and cook, stirring, for 1 minute. Gradually stir in the stock or water and bring to the boil. Lower the heat, cover and simmer for about 15 minutes. Adjust the seasoning. Serve with bread.

ELIZABETH HODGKIN • HEADINGTON, OXFORDSHIRE

Creamy Potato, Parsnip and Butter Bean Soup

Serves 4-6

I like to serve this tasty vegan soup with homemade wholemeal bread.

15 ml (1 tbsp) vegetable margarine
1 large onion, chopped
3-4 garlic cloves, chopped
2 large parsnips
3 medium potatoes
425 g (15 oz) can butter beans
600 ml (1 pint) water
7.5 ml (1½ tsp) vegan or vegetable bouillon
3 bay leaves
pinch of dried oregano
15 ml (1 tbsp) lemon juice
300 ml (½ pint) soya milk (unsweetened)
salt and freshly ground black pepper

Melt the margarine in a large saucepan. Add the onion and garlic and sauté until the onion is softened. Meanwhile, peel and roughly chop the parsnips and potatoes. Add to the saucepan and stir well.

Add the butter beans with their liquid, and the water. Add the vegan or vegetable bouillon, bay leaves, oregano and lemon juice. Bring to the boil, lower the heat, cover and simmer for 20-30 minutes or until the vegetables are softened. Remove from the heat and discard the bay leaves. Stir in the soya milk.

Pureé the soup, in batches if necessary, in a blender or food processor until smooth. If the soup is too thick add a little more water. Reheat if necessary and adjust the seasoning before serving.

C. MOORE • BELFAST

Turkish Lentil Soup

Serves 4-6

An authentic Turkish soup, which is quick and easy to make. It is delicious served as a warming lunch with crusty French bread, or in smaller quantities as an unusual starter. As an alternative to lemon, sprinkle each portion of soup with a little finely grated Cheddar or Gruyère before serving.

25 g (1 oz) butter or margarine
2 large onions, chopped
2 garlic cloves, crushed
15-25 g (½-1 oz) plain flour
1 litre (1¾ pints) hot vegetable stock
4 large tomatoes, chopped
25 g (1 oz) tomato purée
salt and freshly ground black pepper
250 g (9 oz) red lentils, well rinsed
lemon juice to taste

TO GARNISH:
lemon slices

Melt the butter in a large saucepan, add the onions and garlic and fry gently until softened. Add just enough flour to absorb the fat and cook, stirring, for 1 minute. Gradually stir in the vegetable stock, then add the chopped tomatoes, tomato purée and seasoning.

Bring to the boil, then add the lentils. When the mixture returns to the boil lower the heat, cover and simmer for 30 minutes, stirring regularly.

If the soup is too thick, add a little more water. Check the seasoning. Add a squeeze of lemon juice to each portion, sprinkle with pepper and top with a lemon slice before serving.

CAROLINE BENTLEY • MAIDSTONE, KENT

Almond and Celery Soup

Serves 4-6

*A delicious celery soup flavoured with sweet almonds. Serve with crusty wholemeal
bread or croûtons.*

75 g (3 oz) blanched almonds, chopped
1 head of celery, trimmed and chopped
1 small onion, chopped
900 ml (1½ pints) light vegetable stock
25 g (1 oz) butter
25 g (1 oz) flour
300 ml (½ pint) milk
salt and freshly ground black pepper
50 ml (2 fl oz) single cream (optional)

TO GARNISH:
toasted shredded almonds

Put the almonds, celery, onion and stock in a large saucepan. Bring to the boil,
lower the heat, cover and simmer gently for about 1½ hours. Purée the soup in a
blender or food processor.

Melt the butter in a clean saucepan. Stir in the flour and cook, stirring, for
1 minute. Gradually stir in the puréed vegetable mixture and milk. Bring to the
boil, stirring continuously. Remove from the heat, adjust the seasoning and stir
in the cream, if liked. Serve sprinkled with toasted shredded almonds.

Pumpkin Soup with Cheese Croûtons

Serves 8

I always enjoy this nutritious, warming soup in the autumn, with freshly baked bread rolls. Pumpkin is a particularly useful ingredient, since it is inexpensive and available almost worldwide.

30 ml (2 tbsp) olive oil
1 onion, finely sliced
1 kg (2¼ lb) pumpkin flesh, cut into chunks
finely grated rind and juice of 1 orange
pinch of ground cinnamon
salt and freshly ground black pepper
2 litres (3½ pints) vegetable stock
100 ml (3½ fl oz) single cream
freshly grated nutmeg
30 ml (2 tbsp) snipped chives

FOR THE CROÛTONS:
30 g (1¼ oz) butter
15 ml (1 tbsp) olive oil
200 g (7 oz) stale bread, cubed
150 g (5 oz) Appenzell cheese, grated
50 ml (2 fl oz) single cream

Heat the oil in a large saucepan, add the onion and cook gently until softened. Add the pumpkin, orange rind and juice, cinnamon and salt and pepper to taste. Cover and cook gently for 10 minutes. Add about three quarters of the stock, and simmer for 15 minutes or until the pumpkin is soft and tender.

Pour the mixture into a blender or food processor and blend until smooth, then return the soup to the pan. Add the cream, together with a little more stock if necessary to thin, then correct the seasoning, adding a little nutmeg. Keep hot.

To make the croûtons, melt the butter and oil together in a frying pan, add the bread cubes and fry until golden brown. Sprinkle the cheese on top of the croûtons. Add the cream and turn the croûtons to coat in cream and cheese.

Pour the soup into warmed bowls, and divide the croûtons between them. Sprinkle the chives over the soup, and serve immediately.

ANTON MOSIMANN

Vichyssoise Soup

Serves 4-6

This delicious leek soup is equally good served hot or cold. If you intend to serve it cold, soften the vegetables in 30 ml (2 tbsp) oil rather than butter.

4 large leeks
25 g (1 oz) butter
1 small onion, chopped
3 medium potatoes, peeled and sliced
1.2 litres (2 pints) vegetable stock
salt and freshly ground black pepper
50 ml (2 fl oz) single cream

To GARNISH:
chopped parsley

Trim the leeks, wash thoroughly, then chop roughly. Melt the butter in a large saucepan, add the leeks and onion and cook gently for about 5 minutes until softened.

Add the potatoes and mix well, then stir in the stock. Bring to the boil. Cover and simmer for about 30 minutes, stirring occasionally, until the potatoes are soft. Purée the soup in a blender or food processor until smooth.

Either return the soup to the pan and heat through; or pour into a tureen and allow to cool, then chill thoroughly.

Before serving, add salt and pepper to taste and stir in the cream. Serve sprinkled with chopped parsley.

THE DEAN OF BELFAST

Fresh Corn Soup

Serves 4

This soup comes from Guatemala, where it is usually eaten with tortillas. You can use frozen sweetcorn kernels instead of fresh corn but the flavour won't be quite as good.

2-3 corn cobs
250 ml (8 fl oz) water
50 g (2 oz) margarine or butter
1 small onion, very finely chopped
50 g (2 oz) flour
600 ml (1 pint) milk
2.5 ml (½ tsp) salt
freshly ground black pepper

Cut the sweetcorn kernels from the cobs and place them in a saucepan with the water. Bring to the boil, lower the heat and simmer, covered, for about 10 minutes until the corn is just tender.

Melt the margarine or butter in another saucepan. Add the onion and cook gently until softened. Stir in the flour and cook, stirring, for 1 minute. Gradually add the milk, stirring constantly. Add the corn, together with the cooking water, and season with salt and pepper to taste.

Bring to the boil to thicken, stirring all the time. Cook gently for 2-3 minutes, then taste and adjust the seasoning before serving.

Iced Herb Soup

Serves 6

*This soup is particularly refreshing and delicious chilled. I like to serve it with
wholemeal croûtons, flavoured with sesame seeds.*

**15 ml (1 tbsp) olive oil
1 onion, chopped
350 g (12 oz) potatoes, peeled and diced
1.2 litres (2 pints) water
3-4 parsley sprigs, stalks removed
2 mint sprigs, stems removed
6-8 chives
salt and freshly ground black pepper
150 ml (¼ pint) single cream**

Heat the oil in a large saucepan, add the onion and cook gently, covered, for
10 minutes. Stir in the potatoes and cook, stirring occasionally, for 5 minutes.
Add the water and bring to the boil. Lower the heat and simmer, covered, for
30 minutes or until the potatoes are tender. Remove from the heat and set aside
to cool.

Work the cooled mixture in a blender or food processor together with the
herbs until smooth and creamy. If necessary, thin the soup with a little more
water. Season liberally with salt and pepper. Cover and chill in the refrigerator
until required.

To serve, ladle the soup into chilled bowls and swirl a spoonful of cream on
each portion. Serve with wholemeal croûtons or crusty bread.

ROSE ELLIOT

Snacks
& Starters

Tomatoes with Guacamole

Serves 4

This pretty starter is good served with tortilla chips or homemade Melba toast. To make Melba toast, toast slices of bread in the usual way, then slice each piece horizontally in half so that you end up with two thin slices. Cut these across diagonally, then lay them on a grill pan and grill for a minute or two until they become crisp, lightly browned and curl up at the edges.

5 medium tomatoes
1 large or 2 small ripe avocados
1 garlic clove, crushed
1 green chilli
juice of 1 lime
salt and freshly ground black pepper

To GARNISH:
few coriander leaves (optional)

Skin one of the tomatoes by immersing it in boiling water for a minute or two, then peeling away the skin with a sharp knife. Quarter, deseed and chop the tomato. Peel, halve and stone the avocado(s) and cut the flesh into rough chunks. Put the avocado chunks into a blender or food processor, with the chopped tomato and garlic.

Halve the chilli and remove the seeds, taking care to wash your hands afterwards. Add the chilli, or part of it, to the avocado, along with 15 ml (1 tbsp) of the lime juice and a little salt and pepper. Whizz the mixture until it's smooth, then taste, and add more chilli, lime juice and salt and pepper, as desired.

Slice the remaining tomatoes into thin rounds and arrange these on 4 serving plates. Spoon the avocado mixture on top. If available, snip some fresh coriander leaves over the guacamole.

ROSE ELLIOT

Mushroom Pâté

Serves 3

Served on a few leaves of lettuce or watercress, garnished with slices of lemon and accompanied with crisp Melba toast, this tasty pâté makes a pleasant first course. It's also delicious served with a creamy mustard sauce, made by mixing a spoonful or two of Dijon mustard into a carton of soured cream. It's good as a sandwich filling too, with soft, light bread.

450 g (1 lb) button mushrooms
50 g (2 oz) butter
1 garlic clove, crushed
salt and freshly ground black pepper

TO SERVE:
a few lettuce leaves
chopped chives
lemon slices

Wash the mushrooms, then pat them dry and cut into slices. Heat the butter in a large saucepan and add the mushrooms and the garlic. Cook over a moderate heat until any moisture released by the mushrooms has evaporated and they are dry and buttery. This may take 15-20 minutes.

Then purée the mushrooms in a food processor or blender. Season with salt and pepper to taste and press the mixture into a small bowl, pâté dish or tin. Leave to cool.

To serve the pâté, put a few crisp lettuce leaves or watercress sprigs on individual plates and arrange a couple of slices of the pâté on the plates. Sprinkle with chopped chives and garnish with lemon slices.

ROSE ELLIOT

Chick Pea and Spinach Pâté

Serves 4

An incredibly quick and easy vegetarian pâté!

125 g (4 oz) canned chick peas, drained
1 onion, finely chopped
450 g (1 lb) spinach, washed and finely chopped
1 garlic clove
30 ml (2 tbsp) chopped coriander
10 ml (2 tsp) chopped mint
5 ml (1 tsp) turmeric
2.5 ml (½ tsp) ground cumin
30 ml (2 tbsp) olive oil
30 ml (2 tbsp) lemon juice
2.5 ml (½ tsp) finely grated lemon rind
salt and freshly ground black pepper

Put all of the ingredients in a blender or food processor, adding salt and pepper to taste, and work until evenly mixed and smooth. Spread the mixture in a small bowl or pâté dish. Serve with wholemeal toast or crusty bread.

SUE GREIG • OXFORD

Glazed Vegetable Pastries

Serves 6

Serve these tasty mixed vegetable pastries as a snack, starter or accompaniment to main dishes. You can use any mixture of baby vegetables: try mangetout, baby corn and carrots, for example.

six 10 cm (4 inch) squares of filo pastry
25 g (1 oz) butter, melted
350 g (12 oz) mixed baby vegetables
salt and freshly ground black pepper
60 ml (4 tbsp) lemon mayonnaise
15 ml (1 tbsp) chopped mixed herbs, eg chives, parsley and chervil
50 g (2 oz) fresh soft goat's cheese
a little single cream

Preheat the oven to 190°C (375°F) mark 5. Place each filo pastry square over a buttered upturned Yorkshire pudding tin and brush liberally with melted butter. Bake in the oven for 7-8 minutes until crisp and golden. Carefully lift each pastry basket off the tin and place on a wire rack.

Meanwhile, cook the vegetables in boiling salted water until just tender; drain well. In a bowl, beat the mayonnaise with the herbs and goat's cheese until evenly blended. Add enough cream to give a coating consistency.

Place the pastry cases on a baking sheet and divide the vegetables between them. Spoon the cheese mixture over the vegetables and place under a hot grill for about 1 minute to glaze. Serve immediately.

MOYRA FRASER • GOOD HOUSEKEEPING

Stuffed Mushrooms

Serves 4

Tasty stuffed mushrooms with a cheesy breadcrumb filling served on fried croûtes.

4 large cup mushrooms
15 g (½ oz) butter
30 ml (2 tbsp) freshly grated Parmesan or Cheddar cheese
5 ml (1 tsp) chopped parsley
30 ml (2 tbsp) fresh breadcrumbs
salt and freshly ground black pepper
a little milk to mix
15-30 ml (1-2 tbsp) toasted breadcrumbs

TO SERVE:
4 fried bread croûtes

Preheat the oven to 180°C (350°F) mark 4. Trim the stalks from the mushroom caps and place cup-side up in a greased baking tin. Chop the stalks.

Melt the butter in a saucepan, add the chopped mushroom stalks and sauté gently for a few minutes. Stir in the cheese, parsley, fresh breadcrumbs, salt and pepper, then add enough milk to bind the mixture. Cook very gently for a few minutes until the breadcrumbs are swollen.

Divide the stuffing between the mushrooms and sprinkle with the toasted breadcrumbs. Cover with a sheet of greased greaseproof paper and bake in the oven for 15 minutes. Serve immediately on the croûtes.

MRS O. WHITE

Swiss Mushrooms

Serves 4

450 g (1 lb) large button mushrooms
30 ml (2 tbsp) lemon juice
salt and freshly ground black pepper
about 40 g (1½ oz) Gruyère or Cheddar cheese, grated
200 ml (⅓ pint) single cream
1 egg yolk

Preheat the oven to 220°C (425°F) mark 7. Remove the stalks from the mushrooms. Wipe the mushroom caps and place in a large shallow pan with the lemon juice over a low heat. Cover and cook gently for 10 minutes.

Transfer the mushrooms to a greased baking dish, placing them cap-side down. Season with a little salt and pepper to taste, then sprinkle with grated cheese. Mix the cream with the egg yolk and carefully pour around the mushrooms. Bake in the preheated oven for about 10-15 minutes until the cheese is golden brown and bubbling. Serve immediately.

SARA TURNER

Pumpkin Pancakes

Makes 12

250 g (9 oz) pumpkin flesh
25 g (1 oz) sugar
2 eggs
50 g (2 oz) self-raising flour
pinch of ground allspice
oil for frying

Cut the pumpkin into even-sized pieces and cook in boiling salted water for about 15 minutes until tender. Drain thoroughly and transfer to a blender or food processor. Add the sugar, eggs, flour and allspice, and work to a smooth purée.

Heat a little oil in a frying pan until smoking. Add spoonfuls of the pumpkin mixture, spacing them a little apart, and fry over moderate heat until golden. Turn and cook the other side. Drain on absorbent kitchen paper. Repeat until all the mixture is used. Serve warm, with honey.

FLOELLA BENJAMIN

Pakoras

Serves 4

Delicious deep-fried vegetable morsels in a spicy batter. Choose from the vegetables suggested below, or use a mixture; you will need about 225 g (8 oz) in total. If you use onions, add them to the batter in teaspoonfuls.

FOR THE BATTER:
65 g (2½ oz) gram flour (besan)
7.5 ml (1½ tsp) turmeric
pinch of bicarbonate of soda
5 ml (1 tsp) black onion seed or onion powder
100-120 ml (3½-4 fl oz) water
7.5 ml (1½ tsp) finely grated fresh root ginger
pinch of salt (optional)
oil for deep-frying

FOR THE VEGETABLES:
thinly sliced potatoes
aubergine slices, about 5 mm (¼ inch) thick
cauliflower florets
spinach leaves
chopped onions

To make the batter, sift the flour, turmeric, bicarbonate of soda and black onion seed into a bowl. Gradually stir in the water and beat the mixture to a thick paste. Stir in the ginger and salt if desired.

Heat the oil in a deep-fat fryer until it is very hot. Dip the vegetables into the batter, then deep-fry in the hot oil until crisp and lightly browned. Drain on absorbent kitchen paper and serve immediately.

Cheese Ramekins

Serves 2

2 egg yolks
150 ml (¼ pint) double cream
30 ml (2 tbsp) freshly grated Parmesan cheese
salt and freshly ground black pepper
pinch of mustard powder

Preheat the oven to 180°C (350°F) mark 4. Put all the ingredients in a bowl and beat until evenly mixed. Divide between two ramekin dishes and place in a bain marie or roasting tin containing enough water to come halfway up the sides of the ramekins. Cook in the oven for 25 minutes. Serve immediately, with toast or crusty bread.

MARCHIONESS OF DUFFERIN AND AVA

Cheese and Potato Balls

Serves 4

225 g (8 oz) potatoes
25 g (1 oz) butter
50 g (2 oz) Cheddar or Gruyère cheese, grated
salt and freshly ground black pepper
1 egg, beaten
breadcrumbs for coating
oil for deep-frying

Cut the potatoes into even-sized pieces and cook in boiling salted water until tender; drain. Mash the potatoes with the butter, cheese and salt and pepper to taste. Add a little of the beaten egg to bind the mixture. Form the mixture into small balls, about 2.5 cm (1 inch) in diameter.

Heat the oil in a deep-fat fryer. Dip the potato balls in the remaining beaten egg, then coat with breadcrumbs. Deep-fry the potato balls in the hot oil until crisp and lightly browned. Drain on absorbent kitchen paper and serve immediately, on cocktail sticks if you prefer.

Victoria Wood's Best Sandwich Ever

Serves 1

I like to use good wholemeal bread – preferably with bits in! If you live near one of the few places that sells alfalfa sprouts, do include them.

**2 large slices wholemeal bread
butter for spreading**

FOR THE FILLING:
**avocado, tomato and cucumber slices
cress and alfalfa sprouts (if available)
mayonnaise
salt and freshly ground black pepper**

Spread the bread slices with butter. Sandwich them together with lots of avocado, tomato, cucumber, cress and alfalfa sprouts, putting mayonnaise and seasoning in the middle. Eat it!

VICTORIA WOOD

Salads

Vitality Salad Lunch

Serves 1

This is a crunchy, health-giving salad based on sprouted beans and seeds, which you can buy, ready to use, in some supermarkets and health shops. Alternatively you can make them at home – see below. Apart from the sprouted beans, you can really throw in any fresh vegetables that you fancy: grated carrots are always good, and I like to add some kind of green leafy vegetables, as well as plenty of chopped fresh herbs. This salad is lovely topped with a creamy dollop of houmus or mashed avocado.

a handful of sprouted beans
1 carrot, coarsely grated
1 small raw beetroot, grated
3-4 tender spinach or lettuce leaves, or some watercress, shredded
1 tomato, chopped
small piece of cucumber, diced
chopped herbs as available, ie mint or basil, parsley and chives
5-10 ml (1-2 tsp) olive oil
squeeze of lemon juice
sea salt
4 spoonfuls of houmus, guacamole or mashed avocado

Put the sprouted beans into a bowl with the carrot, beetroot, shredded leaves, tomato and cucumber. Add some of the chopped herbs, reserving some to sprinkle on top at the end. Add the olive oil, lemon juice and sea salt to taste. Mix lightly.

Spoon the mixture onto a plate or deep dish, top with the houmus, guacamole or mashed avocado, and sprinkle with the remaining chopped herbs.

HOW TO SPROUT BEANS AND SEEDS

A mixture of different beans and seeds is pleasant in a salad, I like little green mung beans and whole lentils. Take a tablespoon each of mung beans and whole lentils, and soak them in cold water overnight. Next day put them into a sieve, or a jar with a piece of gauze secured over the top with an elastic band. Rinse them under the tap if they are in a sieve, or, if you are using the jar method, by filling the jar with cold water, then pouring it out through the gauze, which will prevent the beans from coming out too. Shake off any excess water, then just leave the beans for 3-4 days to sprout, rinsing them as described twice a day. This makes enough for about 4 Vitality Salads; once they have sprouted, the beans will keep in the refrigerator for several days without further rinsing and draining.

ROSE ELLIOT

Middle Eastern Carrot Salad

Serves 2-3

A purée of cooked carrots enlivened with lemon juice, olive oil, pine nuts and flat-leaf parsley, this can be served on its own as a first course, or as a dip with crudités, or as part of a mixed salad plate with other raw vegetables.

450 g (1 lb) carrots
15 ml (1 tbsp) olive oil
juice of 1 lemon, or to taste
sea salt and freshly ground black pepper
25 g (1 oz) pine nuts

To GARNISH:
flat-leaf parsley or watercress sprigs

Cut the carrots into even-sized pieces and steam or boil for about 15 minutes until tender. Drain, then put them into a bowl. Mash the carrots fairly finely with the oil, then mix in lemon juice and salt and pepper to taste. Beat well, then leave to cool. Serve on a flat plate, sprinkled with pine nuts. Arrange sprigs of flat-leaf parsley or watercress around the outside.

ROSE ELLIOT

Carrot and Banana Salad

Serves 4

This salad makes a lovely lunch, served with light, crumbly homemade wholemeal bread. Carrots are a marvellous standby all the year – hot or cold, cooked or raw, whole or grated they are a thoroughly versatile vegetable. They're also very nourishing, being rich in vitamins A and C.

50 g (2 oz) raisins
2 large carrots, peeled and grated
4 large bananas, peeled and sliced
juice of ½ orange

FOR THE DRESSING:
225 g (8 oz) cottage cheese
150 ml (¼ pint) milk, top of the milk or cream

TO GARNISH:
chopped walnuts

Wash the raisins, place in a bowl and pour over hot water to cover. Leave to plump for 10 minutes, then drain. Mix the raisins with the carrots, bananas and orange juice. Arrange on a serving plate. To make the dressing, blend the cottage cheese with the milk or cream in a blender or food processor until smooth. Pour over the carrot salad and sprinkle with chopped walnuts to serve.

ROSE ELLIOT

Mixed Salad with Parmesan Cheese

Serves 3-4

A crunchy salad of cabbage, carrot, onion and tomatoes in a lemon and oil dressing, topped with freshly grated Parmesan.

1 onion, thinly sliced
175 g (6 oz) cabbage, shredded
2 carrots, finely sliced
6-8 tomatoes, chopped

FOR THE DRESSING:
60 ml (2 fl oz) olive oil
60 ml (2 fl oz) lemon juice
30 ml (2 tbsp) white wine vinegar
5 ml (1 tsp) salt
1.25 ml (¼ tsp) coarsely ground black pepper
1 garlic clove, crushed

TO SERVE:
50 g (2 oz) Parmesan cheese, freshly grated

Combine the onion, cabbage, carrots and tomatoes in a salad bowl. Put the ingredients for the dressing in a screw-topped jar and shake well to mix. Pour the dressing over the salad and sprinkle with the grated Parmesan to serve.

Curried Wild Rice Salad

Serves 8

Wild rice has a delicious nutty flavour and chewy texture making it perfect for salads. It isn't in fact a type of rice at all, but rather a small dark brown grain.

350 g (12 oz) wild rice
salt and freshly ground black pepper
½ green pepper, seeded and chopped
2-3 celery sticks, chopped
4 spring onions, finely chopped
25 g (1 oz) parsley, finely chopped
1 lettuce

FOR THE DRESSING:
125 ml (4 fl oz) sunflower oil
60 ml (2 fl oz) lemon juice
60 ml (2 fl oz) red wine vinegar
5 ml (1 tsp) chopped mint
5 ml (1 tsp) chopped dill
5 ml (1 tsp) snipped chives
3.75 ml (¾ tsp) Dijon mustard
2.5 ml (½ tsp) curry powder

Rinse the wild rice in cold water, then place in a large saucepan with approximately 4 times the volume of cold water. Add salt, bring to the boil, cover and simmer for 25-30 minutes until tender. Drain and rinse under running cold water. Drain thoroughly.

Combine the wild rice, green pepper, celery, spring onions and chopped parsley in a bowl and stir lightly to mix evenly. Separate the lettuce leaves and use to line a salad bowl. Spoon the rice salad into the bowl.

To make the dressing, put all the ingredients in a screw-topped jar with salt and pepper to taste. Shake vigorously to mix, then pour over the salad.

Asparagus Salad

Serves 4

An oriental-style salad featuring asparagus in a piquant soy and sesame dressing. You can use olive oil in place of sesame for a milder flavour.

900 g (2 lb) asparagus
salt and freshly ground black pepper

FOR THE DRESSING:
30 ml (2 tbsp) soy sauce
15 ml (1 tbsp) sesame oil
2.5 ml (½ tsp) sugar

TO SERVE:
lettuce or other salad leaves

Cut off the tough part of the asparagus stems and discard. Cut diagonally into 2.5 cm (1 inch) pieces. Cook in boiling salted water for 3 minutes only. Drain and allow to cool.

To make the dressing, mix the soy sauce, oil and sugar together in a shallow dish. Add the asparagus, cover and leave to marinate in the refrigerator for at least 1 hour. Check the seasoning.

To serve, arrange the lettuce or other salad leaves on individual plates and top with the asparagus.

Pear and Cream Cheese Salad

Serves 4

This refreshing salad should be served very cold. It makes a delicious light starter.

4 ripe dessert pears
lemon juice for sprinkling
25 g (1 oz) Roquefort cheese
knob of butter
75 g (3 oz) cream cheese
a little cream or milk
4 lettuce leaves
paprika for dusting

Peel the pears, halve and carefully remove the cores. Sprinkle with a little lemon juice to prevent discoloration. Cream the Roquefort cheese with the butter and place a spoonful in the middle of each pear half. Thin the cream cheese with a little cream or milk.

Place a lettuce leaf on each serving plate. Place a pear on each lettuce leaf and coat with the cream cheese. Dust with paprika and serve.

BRIAN RIX

Roasted Pepper, Aubergine and Artichoke Salad

Serves 3-4

This recipe is based on Italian-style roast peppers. It has simply evolved and grown with time! Serve it with chunks of French bread or crusty wholemeal bread.

1 large green pepper
1 large red pepper
1 large yellow pepper
1 medium aubergine
3-4 garlic cloves, sliced or chopped
salt and freshly ground black pepper
chopped fresh or dried oregano or marjoram
extra virgin olive oil for cooking
400 g (14 oz) can artichoke hearts, drained and chopped
8 black olives

Preheat the oven to 230°C (450°F) mark 8. Halve the peppers, discard the core and seeds, then slice the flesh. Discard the ends from the aubergine, then cut into 1 cm (½ inch) cubes. Put the peppers, aubergine and garlic in a roasting tin and season with salt and pepper. Sprinkle with oregano or marjoram to taste. Baste liberally with olive oil. Roast in the preheated oven for 20 minutes, turning and basting frequently, and adding more oil as necessary.

Lower the temperature to 180°C (350°F) mark 4 and bake for a further 20-30 minutes until the vegetables are tender and just browning, adding the artichoke hearts and olives for the last 10 minutes. Baste frequently during cooking, adding more oil as necessary. Allow to cool completely before serving, with plenty of bread.

JANE BAKER • CARMARTHEN, DYFED

Village Salad

Serves 4

A simple Cypriot salad which is ideal as a light lunch served with plenty of warm pitta bread or crusty wholemeal bread.

handful of lettuce leaves
1 onion, thinly sliced
1 large cucumber, or 2-3 small ones, chopped
2-3 medium tomatoes, chopped
few black olives

FOR THE DRESSING:
olive oil
lemon juice
salt and freshly ground black pepper
chopped or dried mint

TO SERVE:
50 g (2 oz) feta cheese

Combine the lettuce, onion, cucumber, tomatoes and olives in a large bowl. Add oil, lemon juice, seasoning and mint to taste. Toss lightly to mix. Crumble the feta cheese on top to serve.

Celery and Avocado Salad

Serves 2-4

Serve this Chilean salad as a side salad, or snack with plenty of crusty bread.

**1 head of celery
2 medium ripe avocados**

**FOR THE DRESSING:
juice of 1 lemon
60 ml (4 tbsp) olive oil
salt and freshly ground black pepper**

Discard the coarse outer stalks of the celery. Thinly slice the inner stalks and place on a serving platter. Halve the avocados, discarding the stones, then peel and cut into thick slices. Arrange the avocado slices on top of the celery.

To make the dressing, in a bowl whisk the lemon juice with the oil and seasoning to taste, to form a thick emulsion. Drizzle the dressing over the salad and serve immediately.

Apple and Fennel Salad

Serves 4-6

*This is my own recipe which I have been making for the past 40 years or so! I like
to serve it with a crisp green leafy salad.*

2 eating apples
1 very small fennel bulb
2 onions, diced
2-3 large tomatoes or 2 beef tomatoes
10 ml (2 tsp) caster sugar
salt and freshly ground black pepper

TO GARNISH:
basil sprigs

Quarter, core and dice the apples. Halve the fennel and slice thinly. Mix the
apples with the fennel and onions.

Thinly slice the tomatoes and arrange over the base of a serving plate.
Sprinkle with the sugar, then salt and pepper to taste. Spoon the apple and
fennel mixture on top. Cover and chill the salad in the refrigerator for several
hours before serving, garnished with basil.

MARGERY ROOK • BLACKPOOL, LANCASHIRE

Vegetable
Accompaniments

Beetroot Julienne with Caraway

Serves 4

I love beetroot which I think is one of our most under-used and under-valued vegetables. Cooked like this, it makes a good accompaniment to many main courses. I particularly like it with crisp nut or lentil burgers, along with some creamy light mashed potato. Although I prefer to cook the beetroot myself, when pressed for time, ready-cooked vacuum-packed beetroot is an alternative. Avoid the type with vinegar and preservatives added.

4 raw beetroots
15 g (½ oz) butter
5 ml (1 tsp) caraway seeds
squeeze of lemon juice
sea salt and freshly ground black pepper

If the beetroots have stems and leaves attached, cut these off about 10 cm (4 inches) from the beets. Put the beetroots in a saucepan, add water to cover and bring to the boil. Cook for 1-1½ hours, or until the beetroot are tender when pierced with a sharp knife. Let them cool, then slip off the skins. Slice the beetroots and cut into matchsticks.

Melt the butter in a large saucepan and add the caraway seeds. Stir over the heat for a few seconds, to release the flavour of the caraway, then add the beetroot and stir-fry for a few minutes, until the beetroot is heated through. Add a squeeze of lemon juice and salt and pepper to taste. Serve immediately.

ROSE ELLIOT

Cabbage with Garlic Butter

Serves 4

This is a delicious way to serve cabbage. Choose a Savoy, Primo or January King type.

1 medium-large cabbage, weighing about 700 g (1½ lb)
3 large garlic cloves
50 g (2 oz) butter
sea salt and freshly ground black pepper
freshly grated nutmeg
good squeeze of lemon juice

Wash the cabbage, removing any tough leaves. Cut the cabbage into quarters, cutting out the tough stem, and shred the leaves. Bring 2.5 cm (1 inch) of water to the boil in a large saucepan and add the cabbage. Cover, then boil for 3-4 minutes, or until the cabbage is just tender.

Meanwhile, crush the garlic and mix with the butter. Drain the cabbage, then add the garlic butter with salt, pepper, nutmeg and a good squeeze of lemon juice to taste. Serve at once.

ROSE ELLIOT

Brussels Chicory

Serves 4

A versatile accompaniment which goes well with many main course dishes.

450 g (1 lb) chicory
juice of ½ lemon
50 g (2 oz) butter
125 ml (4 fl oz) milk
salt and freshly ground black pepper
freshly grated nutmeg

Cut off the base of each chicory bulb and remove the bitter core. Discard any discoloured pieces and wash the chicory in cold water; drain. Quarter each bulb lengthwise, then slice into 2.5 cm (1 inch) pieces.

Bring 300 ml (½ pint) water to the boil in a saucepan, with the lemon juice added. Put the chicory into the pan, bring to the boil, then take off the heat and leave for 5 minutes. Drain in a colander and rinse under cold running water. Drain well.

Heat the butter and milk in a saucepan. Add the chicory, salt, pepper and nutmeg to taste. Cover and bring to the boil. Lower the heat and cook gently until the chicory is just tender. Drain and serve immediately.

BELGIAN EMBASSY

Carrot and Parsnip Julienne

Serves 6

The maple syrup glaze lends a rich finishing touch to these vegetables. You can use thin honey instead of maple syrup if you prefer.

450 g (1 lb) carrots
450 g (1 lb) parsnips
75 ml (5 tbsp) orange juice
75 ml (5 tbsp) water
25 g (1 oz) butter
15 ml (1 tbsp) lemon juice
2.5 ml (½ tsp) ground ginger
5 ml (1 tsp) freshly grated nutmeg
pinch of salt
freshly ground black pepper
30 ml (2 tbsp) maple syrup

Peel and trim the carrots and parsnips, then cut into julienne strips, about 5 cm (2 inches) long. Put the vegetable julienne in a heavy-based saucepan with the orange juice, water, butter, lemon juice, ginger, nutmeg, salt, and pepper to taste. Cover and bring to the boil. Lower the heat and simmer for about 15 minutes, until the vegetables are tender.

Uncover and drizzle with the maple syrup. Increase the heat and cook, stirring gently, until the vegetables are glazed. Serve immediately.

Cabbage in Tomato Sauce

Serves 4

This simple cabbage recipe from Malawi goes well with many main dishes. As a variation, mix 45 ml (3 tbsp) crunchy peanut butter with the water before adding to the cabbage.

15 ml (1 tbsp) oil
1 onion, chopped
3 tomatoes, skinned and sliced
¼ medium cabbage, cut into small pieces
salt and freshly ground black pepper
125 ml (4 fl oz) water

Heat the oil in a saucepan, add the onion and cook until softened and lightly browned. Stir in the tomatoes, cover and simmer for 3 minutes. Add the cabbage, cover and cook over a low heat for 5 minutes.

Season the cabbage mixture with salt and pepper and stir in the water. Cover and cook gently for 10-15 minutes until the cabbage is tender. Serve immediately.

Aubergines in Coconut

Serves 4

An unusual accompaniment featuring aubergine spiced with chilli, baked in creamy coconut milk. Use fresh or canned coconut milk.

2 large aubergines
4 onions, chopped
1 chilli pepper, finely chopped
1 thyme sprig
600 ml (1 pint) coconut milk
salt (optional)

Preheat the oven to 180°C (350°F) mark 4. Trim the ends off the aubergines, then cut into thin slices and place in a large shallow ovenproof dish. Sprinkle the onions, chilli pepper and thyme over the aubergine slices and pour on the coconut milk. Add salt if preferred. Cover and cook in the oven for 50 minutes, removing the lid for the last 10 minutes to brown the top. Serve hot.

FLOELLA BENJAMIN

Sweet Potato Casserole

Serves 4-6

A delicious accompaniment which goes particularly well with spicy dishes.

500 g (1 lb 2 oz) sweet potatoes
125 g (4 oz) butter
3 large bananas, sliced
juice of 2 oranges

Cook the sweet potatoes in their skins in boiling water to cover until just tender. Drain and allow to cool. When cool enough to handle, peel and cut into slices.

Preheat the oven to 180°C (350°F) mark 4. Arrange half of the sweet potato slices in a buttered ovenproof dish in a single layer. Dot with a quarter of the butter, then cover with half of the banana slices. Dot with butter. Repeat these layers, finishing with a layer of banana slices and the remaining butter. Pour on the orange juice and bake in the preheated oven for 30 minutes. Serve hot.

FLOELLA BENJAMIN

Green Beans with Cumin

Serves 6

These mildly spiced beans are an ideal accompaniment to serve with curries and other Indian dishes.

700 g (1½ lb) green beans
450 g (1 lb) tomatoes
45 ml (3 tbsp) oil
1 medium onion, sliced
10 ml (2 tsp) cumin seeds
30 ml (2 tbsp) tomato purée
150 ml (¼ pint) water
salt and freshly ground black pepper

Top and tail the beans; cut them in half if large. Immerse the tomatoes in boiling water for about 30 seconds, then remove and peel away the skins. Chop the tomatoes.

Heat the oil in a sauté pan, add the onion and cook, stirring for 1-2 minutes. Add the green beans and cumin seeds. Sauté, stirring, for a further 2-3 minutes. Stir in the chopped tomatoes, tomato purée and water. Add salt and pepper. Bring to the boil, then lower the heat, cover and simmer for 15 minutes or until the beans are just tender. Adjust the seasoning before serving.

MOYRA FRASER • GOOD HOUSEKEEPING

Aubergine
and Yogurt Relish

Serves 6

This spicy relish is the perfect accompaniment to serve with Fragrant Saffron Pilau (see page 79). As fried aubergines absorb a lot of oil during frying, it's important to drain them well before completing the recipe.

550 g (1¼ lb) aubergines
salt and freshly ground black pepper
10 ml (2 tsp) ground cumin
10 ml (2 tsp) ground coriander
1.25 ml (¼ tsp) chilli powder
about 150 ml (¼ pint) olive oil
150 ml (5 fl oz) natural yogurt
1 clove garlic, crushed
15 ml (1 tbsp) chopped fresh mint

To GARNISH:
mint sprig

Trim the ends off the aubergines, then cut into thin slices. Place in a colander and sprinkle liberally with salt. Leave to stand for 30 minutes. Rinse well, then pat dry with absorbent kitchen paper.

Mix the cumin, coriander and chilli powder together. Heat a little of the oil in a non-stick frying pan. Add enough aubergine slices to form a single layer and sprinkle with the spices. Fry until golden brown and tender, about 2-3 minutes. Drain well on kitchen paper. Repeat with the remaining aubergine slices, adding more oil as necessary. Arrange the aubergine slices in a serving dish.

Mix together the yogurt, garlic, mint and salt and pepper to taste, and spoon over the aubergines. Cover and chill before serving, garnished with mint.

MOYRA FRASER, GOOD HOUSEKEEPING

Green Tomato Sauce

Serves 2-3

I recently invented this sauce to cope with a glut of green tomatoes which would not keep long enough to go red! It goes particularly well with nut roasts.

225 g (8 oz) green tomatoes
50 g (2 oz) onion
50 g (2 oz) green pepper, seeded
15 ml (1 tbsp) olive oil
1 garlic clove, crushed
300 ml (½ pint) vegetable stock
salt and freshly ground black pepper
1 rosemary sprig

Finely chop the green tomatoes, onion and green pepper. Heat the oil in a saucepan. Add the chopped vegetables and crushed garlic and fry gently, turning constantly for 2-3 minutes. Add the stock, seasoning and rosemary. Put a lid on the saucepan and cook gently for 15-20 minutes, or until the vegetables are softened and reduced to a thick sauce.

BARBARA SHAW • OKEHAMPTON, DEVON

Assorted Vegetable Sauté

Serves 6

This colourful stir-fry is popular in Indonesia. Omit the chilli powder for a milder flavour. You can either serve it as an accompaniment or with rice as a light meal.

30 ml (2 tbsp) vegetable or peanut oil
1 small onion, thinly sliced
2 garlic cloves, crushed
2.5 cm (1 inch) piece fresh root ginger, grated
225 g (8 oz) cabbage, coarsely shredded
175 g (6 oz) green beans, chopped
2 carrots, thinly sliced diagonally
½ green pepper, seeded and sliced
5 ml (1 tsp) salt
5 ml (1 tsp) dried red chilli (optional)
15 ml (1 tbsp) brown sugar
1 bay leaf
15-30 ml (1-2 tbsp) soy sauce

Heat the oil in a wok or sauté pan. Add the onion and garlic and stir-fry for 2 minutes. Add the ginger, cabbage, green beans, carrots and green pepper, stirring well. Add the salt, dried chilli if using, sugar and bay leaf. Stir-fry for 5-7 minutes until the vegetables are cooked but still crisp. Stir in the soy sauce and cook, stirring, for 1-2 minutes; do not overcook. Discard the bay leaf. Serve immediately.

Champ

Serves 4

You can also flavour this potato dish with snipped chives, chopped parsley, nettle tops or young green peas. In the latter case, add the cooked whole peas at the end. For a warming supper dish to kindle the coldest heart, serve scrambled eggs sprinkled with chopped parsley in the middle of champ.

700 g (1½ lb) potatoes, peeled
salt and freshly ground black pepper
10 spring onions or 2 leeks, sliced or chopped
about 125 ml (4 fl oz) milk
50 g (2 oz) butter, melted

Cook the potatoes in boiling salted water until tender; drain. Meanwhile put the chopped spring onions or leeks in a saucepan with the milk and simmer gently until tender. Drain, reserving the milk.

Mash the potatoes, add the spring onions and season with salt and pepper to taste. Beat well, adding enough of the hot milk to give a smooth, creamy consistency. Turn into a warmed deep serving dish and make a well in the centre. Pour the hot melted butter into the well and serve immediately.

JEREMY IRONS

Pasta
Dishes

Penne with Onion, Peppers and Aubergine

Serves 4

This is a pleasant combination of flavours and textures. The vegetable part can be prepared in advance, then you can simply reheat it as the pasta cooks and throw the two together for a quick supper dish. A simple mixed salad – torn lettuce leaves, onion rings, a little tomato – makes the ideal accompaniment.

1 large aubergine
sea salt
2 red peppers
1 large onion
30 ml (2 tbsp) olive oil
freshly ground black pepper
350 g (12 oz) penne

TO SERVE:
freshly grated Parmesan cheese (optional)

Cut the aubergine into matchsticks. Put these into a colander, sprinkle with sea salt, and leave on one side to degorge. Meanwhile, cut the peppers into quarters and lay them, skinside uppermost, on a grill pan. Put them under a very hot grill for about 15 minutes, or until the skins are charred and beginning to lift up. Then put the peppers into a bowl and cover. Leave until they're cool enough to handle, then peel off the skin with a sharp knife. Rinse the peppers, pat dry and cut into thin strips.

Cut the onion in half, then slice into half-circles. Heat 15 ml (1 tbsp) of the oil in a large pan, add the onion and fry gently for about 15 minutes, or until brown and softened.

Meanwhile, rinse the aubergine and pat dry. Add to the onion and fry for a further 10 minutes, or until the aubergine is tender. Stir in the peppers, and seasoning to taste. This sauce can now wait until just before you want to serve the pasta.

Cook the pasta in plenty of boiling water until it is al dente (just tender), then drain and return to the still-warm saucepan. Add the remaining 15 ml (1 tbsp) olive oil and some salt and pepper. Meanwhile, heat up the sauce, then add this to the pasta. Toss lightly and serve at once. Hand round Parmesan cheese separately, if you wish.

ROSE ELLIOT

Spaghetti
with Homemade Pesto

Serves 4

Homemade pesto is wonderful, and it's not only good with pasta. Try it spooned over lightly steamed or grilled vegetables, or stirred into vegetable soups. I like to accompany this with a tomato and onion salad, or a simple tomato salad.

a large handful of fresh basil leaves, stems removed
25 g (1 oz) pine nuts
25 g (1 oz) Pecorino or Parmesan cheese, freshly grated
1 garlic clove, sliced
60 ml (4 tbsp) olive oil
350-450 g (12 oz-1 lb) spaghetti
salt and freshly ground black pepper

First, put a large saucepan of water on the hob to heat up for the pasta. Meanwhile, make the pesto. Put the basil leaves into a blender or food processor with the pine nuts, cheese and garlic. Whizz together to make a thick green purée, making sure that all the nuts are blended – scrape down the sides and whizz the mixture several times if necessary. Then add a little of the oil and whizz again. Continue like this until all of the oil is added and the pesto is thick and shiny.

When the water comes to a rolling boil, put in the spaghetti, letting it gradually slip into the water as it softens. When it's all in, give it a quick stir, then boil uncovered for about 10 minutes, until al dente (just tender). Drain into a colander, then return the spaghetti to the still-warm saucepan. Give the pesto a quick stir, then add it to the pasta, mix quickly, season then serve.

ROSE ELLIOT

Vegetable Macaroni Bake

Serves 4-6

I like to serve this pasta bake with a crisp green salad, wholemeal rolls and a glass of sparkling apple juice.

125 g (4 oz) dried red kidney beans, soaked overnight
225 g (8 oz) wholewheat macaroni
salt and freshly ground black pepper
25 g (1 oz) butter or margarine
25 g (1 oz) cornflour
300 ml (½ pint) milk
15 ml (1 tbsp) oil
2 garlic cloves, crushed
1 leek, sliced
1 carrot, chopped
1 courgette, sliced
350 g (12 oz) tomatoes, skinned and chopped
5-10 ml (1-2 tsp) dried basil
125 g (4 oz) Parmesan cheese, freshly grated
2 slices wholemeal bread, crusts removed
125 g (4 oz) Cheddar cheese, grated

Drain the kidney beans, rinse and put into a saucepan with double the volume of water. Bring to the boil, cover and boil vigorously for 10 minutes. Lower the heat and simmer gently for about 1 hour until tender. Drain well.

Meanwhile cook the macaroni in plenty of boiling salted water for 12 minutes; drain thoroughly.

Preheat the oven to 190°C (375°F) mark 5. Melt the butter or margarine in a saucepan, stir in the cornflour, then gradually stir in the milk. Cook, stirring, over a low heat until thickened. Season with salt and pepper to taste.

Heat the oil in another pan, add the garlic, leek, carrot and courgette and fry gently for 5 minutes until softened. Add the tomatoes, basil and kidney beans, then stir into the white sauce with the pasta and Parmesan cheese. Spoon into a greased shallow ovenproof dish.

Work the bread in a food processor or blender to crumbs, or use a grater. Mix the breadcrumbs with the Cheddar cheese and sprinkle over the pasta mixture. Bake in the preheated oven for 30-35 minutes. Serve hot.

SHEILA M. COUSINS • LANCASTER

Celery and Mushroom Pasta

Serves 4-6

Serve this as a meal on its own, or with a side salad.

25 g (1 oz) margarine
1 onion, chopped
2.5 ml (½ tsp) crushed garlic (optional)
4 sticks celery, chopped
225 g (8 oz) large dark mushrooms, roughly chopped
125 g (4 oz) pasta shells
salt and freshly ground black pepper

FOR THE SAUCE:
50 g (2 oz) margarine
50 g (2 oz) wholemeal flour
300 ml (½ pint) milk
300 ml (½ pint) vegetable stock
50 g (2 oz) Gruyère or Cheddar cheese, grated

FOR THE TOPPING:
125 g (4 oz) wholemeal breadcrumbs
125 g (4 oz) Gruyère or Cheddar cheese, grated

Melt the margarine in a pan, add the onion and garlic and fry gently for a few minutes. Add the celery and fry gently for 3-4 minutes. Add the mushrooms to the pan, cover and simmer over a low heat for 10-15 minutes. Meanwhile cook the pasta in plenty of boiling salted water until al dente (just tender); drain thoroughly.

To make the cheese sauce, melt the margarine in a saucepan, then stir in the flour and cook gently for 1 minute. Gradually stir in the milk and stock and cook, stirring, until thickened and smooth. Season with salt and pepper to taste. Remove from the heat and stir in the 50 g (2 oz) cheese.

Mix the cooked pasta into the cheese sauce, then add the cooked vegetables with their juices. Mix the breadcrumbs and cheese for the topping. Spoon the pasta mixture into a large ovenproof dish. Sprinkle on the topping. Bake in the preheated oven for 30 minutes. Serve hot.

ELIZABETH MARSDEN • CRAWLEY, WEST SUSSEX

Vegetable Pastition

Serves 6

This recipe is from the eastern Mediterranean where vegetarian cooking is often the norm, rather than the exception. It provides a balanced meal with natural ingredients. Serve with a large tomato and green salad and good bread, with fruit and perhaps cheese to follow.

225 g (8 oz) pasta shells, bows or spirals
salt and freshly ground black pepper
60 ml (4 tbsp) olive oil
2 garlic cloves, finely chopped
450 g (1 lb) canned or ripe fresh chopped tomatoes
50 g (2 oz) tomato purée
large pinch each of chopped fresh or dried basil, oregano and thyme
1 large onion, chopped
225 g (8 oz) aubergines, roughly chopped
225 g (8 oz) courgettes, roughly chopped
2 eggs
150 ml (5 fl oz) natural yogurt

Preheat the oven to 180°C (350°F) mark 4. Bring a large pan of water to the boil, add the pasta and salt and cook for 3 minutes. Turn off the heat and leave to stand, covered, for 7 minutes. Drain and rinse under cold running water; drain well.

Meanwhile heat half of the oil in a saucepan and fry the garlic until softened. Add the tomatoes, with the tomato purée and herbs. Season generously with salt and pepper and simmer for 10 minutes.

Heat the remaining oil in another pan and fry the onion, aubergines and courgettes for 5 minutes. Spread half of the tomato mixture in an ovenproof dish and cover with the aubergine mixture. Season with salt and pepper then cover with the remaining tomato mixture. Layer the pasta on top. Lightly beat the eggs with the yogurt and spoon over the pasta. Bake in the preheated oven for 45 minutes or until well browned.

MICHAEL BARRY

Vegetable and Noodle Crunch

Serves 4-6

You can adapt this versatile recipe to use different vegetables from any part of the world. I like to serve it with steamed courgettes or broccoli, and a tossed mixed salad.

450 g (1 lb) leeks, trimmed and sliced
salt and freshly ground black pepper
175 g (6 oz) egg noodles
300 ml (½ pint) crème fraîche
small bunch of dill or parsley, finely chopped
225 g (8 oz) button mushrooms, thinly sliced
125 g (4 oz) granary breadcrumbs
50 g (2 oz) Cheddar cheese, finely grated
2 garlic cloves, crushed
25 g (1 oz) butter or margarine, diced

Preheat the oven to 180°C (350°F) mark 4. Cook the leeks in a little water until just tender; drain. Cook the noodles in a large pan of boiling salted water until 'al dente' (just tender); drain well. Mix the crème fraîche with the chopped dill or parsley, then add to the noodles and mix thoroughly. Season with salt and pepper to taste.

Spread half of the mushrooms over the bottom of a deep 18 cm (7 inch) ovenproof dish. Cover with half of the noodles. Place the leeks on top, and cover with the rest of the mushrooms, then the remaining noodles.

Mix the breadcrumbs with the grated cheese and crushed garlic. Mix in the diced butter or margarine. Sprinkle the breadcrumb mixture evenly over the top of the noodles. Bake in the preheated oven for 25-30 minutes. Serve hot.

ROSAMOND RICHARDSON

Pasta with Broccoli

Serves 4

This is based on a traditional recipe from Puglia, the 'heel' of Italy's boot. Don't be shy with the chillies – it's meant to be a lively dish! We are addicted to it. It is best served with a simple rocket salad dressed with oil and a little vinegar.

450 g (1 lb) broccoli
45-60 ml (3-4 tbsp) olive oil
4 garlic cloves, sliced
2 dried red chillies, broken into pieces
salt and freshly ground black pepper
450 g (1 lb) pasta shapes, eg orecchiette or shells

Divide the broccoli into florets and steam, cook in boiling water, or microwave until tender. Drain and refresh under cold running water; set aside.

Heat the olive oil in a saucepan, add the garlic and cook over low to medium heat until softened, but not brown. Add the chillies in small pieces. Add the broccoli and cook over a very low heat for about 15 minutes until it begins to break down. Season with salt and pepper to taste.

Meanwhile, cook the pasta in a large pan of boiling salted water until al dente (just tender); drain thoroughly. Pour the broccoli sauce over the pasta and serve immediately.

LOYD GROSSMAN

Vegetarian Cannelloni

Serves 2-4

I invented this recipe myself as I love cannelloni! Although it sounds fiddly it is in fact quick to prepare – and delicious. A mixed salad of Italian tomatoes, black olives, cucumber, onion and crisp lettuce is the ideal accompaniment. This quantity will serve 2-3 as a main dish, or 4 as a starter.

8 cannelloni tubes (preferably green pasta)
45 ml (3 tbsp) olive or vegetable oil
1 small onion, chopped
125 g (4 oz) mushrooms, chopped
300 g (10 oz) can spinach, drained
10 ml (2 tsp) chopped oregano
10 ml (2 tsp) chopped basil
125 g (4 oz) ricotta cheese, crumbled
30 ml (2 tbsp) tomato purée
salt and freshly ground black pepper
400 g (14 oz) can peeled tomatoes
25 g (1 oz) margarine
25 g (1 oz) plain flour
50 g (2 oz) Cheddar cheese, grated

Preheat the oven to 180°C (350°F) mark 4. Bring a large saucepan of water to the boil and add a drop of oil. Add the cannelloni and boil for 5 minutes; drain.

Heat 30 ml (2 tbsp) oil in a pan, add the onion and fry gently for 2-3 minutes, then add the mushrooms and cook, stirring frequently, until tender. Add the spinach, herbs, ricotta and 15 ml (1 tbsp) tomato purée. Mix well and season with salt and pepper to taste. Cook gently for 5 minutes or until the ricotta is melted and well absorbed. Remove from the heat.

Grease a large rectangular ovenproof dish. Using a teaspoon, carefully fill each cannelloni tube with spinach mixture, holding the other end of the tube against the bottom of the baking dish. (You may have a little filling left over.)

Whizz the tomatoes in a blender or food processor. Melt the margarine in a saucepan. Stir in the flour and cook, stirring, for 1 minute. Gradually stir in the liquidized tomatoes, then the remaining 15 ml (1 tbsp) tomato purée and cook, stirring, for 5 minutes.

Spoon the sauce over the cannelloni and sprinkle with the grated cheese. Bake in the preheated oven for 30 minutes or until the topping is golden.

MRS VAL LANGFORD • ST ALBANS, HERTS

Lasagne

Serves 6-8

A rich authentic lasagne from Italy, featuring ricotta and Romano cheeses. Both cheeses are available from Italian delicatessens; ricotta is also available from larger supermarket cheese counters. If unobtainable substitute cottage cheese for the ricotta, and Parmesan for Romano cheese. You should have enough tomato sauce left over after layering the lasagne to serve as an accompaniment.

FOR THE TOMATO SAUCE:
15 ml (1 tbsp) olive oil
1 small onion, chopped
1 clove garlic, crushed
500 g (1 lb 2 oz) carton passata
1 litre (1¾ pints) water
10 ml (2 tsp) salt
1.25- 2.5 ml (¼-½ tsp) freshly ground black pepper
5 ml (1 tsp) dried basil
5 ml (1 tsp) dried oregano
1 bay leaf
10 ml (2 tsp) sugar
45 ml (3 tbsp) dry red wine (optional)

TO ASSEMBLE:
12 sheets lasagne
225 g (8 oz) mozzarella cheese, grated
700 g (1½ lb) ricotta cheese, grated
50 g (2 oz) Romano cheese, grated
5 ml (1 tsp) chopped fresh parsley
2.5 ml (½ tsp) dried oregano
3 eggs, beaten

TO SERVE:
freshly grated Romano or Parmesan cheese

To make the tomato sauce, heat the olive oil in a saucepan, add the onion and garlic and sauté until softened. Add the passata, water, salt, pepper, herbs, sugar and wine if using. Bring to the boil, partially cover and simmer gently for 2-3 hours.

Preheat the oven to 190°C (375°F) mark 5. Bring a large pan of water to the boil and briefly cook the lasagne sheets; do not overcook. Drain.

Mix two thirds of the grated mozzarella with the ricotta, Romano cheese, parsley, oregano, eggs and seasoning to taste.

Spread a little of the warm tomato sauce over the base of a large rectangular ovenproof dish. Layer a quarter of the lasagne on top of the tomato sauce and cover with a third of the cheese mixture. Drizzle with a little tomato sauce. Repeat the lasagne, cheese mixture and sauce layers twice. Cover with the remaining lasagne. Spread with a generous layer of tomato sauce and top with the remaining mozzarella.

Cover and bake in the preheated oven for 40-45 minutes. Uncover and let stand in a warm place for 15-20 minutes to firm up before serving. Cut into squares. Serve with any remaining tomato sauce, and freshly grated cheese.

Carnival Macaroni Cheese

Serves 4

175 g (6 oz) macaroni
salt and freshly ground black pepper
65 g (2½ oz) butter or margarine
125 g (4 oz) button mushrooms
½ green pepper, seeded and chopped
30 ml (2 tbsp) chopped canned pimento
40 g (1½ oz) flour
375 ml (12 fl oz) milk
125 g (4 oz) Cheddar cheese, grated
50 g (2 oz) Parmesan cheese, freshly grated

FOR THE TOPPING:
40 g (1½ oz) fresh breadcrumbs
a little melted butter

Preheat the oven to 180°C (350°F) mark 4. Bring about 1.2 litres (2 pints) water to the boil in a large saucepan. Add the macaroni and salt. Boil rapidly, stirring, for 2 minutes. Cover the pan, remove from heat and let stand for 10 minutes.

Meanwhile, melt the butter or margarine in a saucepan. Add the mushrooms, green pepper and pimento and sauté until lightly browned. Stir in the flour, salt and pepper to taste. Gradually stir in the milk and cook until thickened, stirring constantly. Add the grated cheeses, stirring until well blended.

Toss the breadcrumbs in the melted butter. Rinse the macaroni with warm water and drain well, then fold into the cheese sauce. Spoon the macaroni cheese into an ovenproof dish and top with the buttered breadcrumbs. Bake in the preheated oven for 25 minutes until the topping is golden brown.

AMERICAN EMBASSY

Pink Pasta

Serves 2-3

This tasty, filling pasta dish is ideal for a quick supper. I like to serve it with a lettuce salad – tossed in a little olive oil and crushed garlic – and sparkling white wine.

150 g (5 oz) broccoli
½ red pepper, cored and seeded
250-300 g (9-10 oz) mushrooms
300 g (10 oz) penne (or other similar pasta)
salt and freshly ground black pepper
45-60 ml (3-4 tbsp) olive oil
2 garlic cloves, crushed or chopped
300 g (10 oz) can chopped tomatoes
10 ml (2 tsp) dried oregano
100 g (3½ oz) low fat soft cream cheese, eg Philadelphia

Chop the broccoli, red pepper and mushrooms into small chunky pieces. Bring a large saucepan of water to the boil for the pasta. Add the penne and salt and boil steadily until al dente (just tender).

Meanwhile, heat the olive oil in a sauté pan, add the vegetables and fry gently for 2-3 minutes. Add the garlic and cook for 1 minute. Stir in the chopped tomatoes, oregano and seasoning to taste. Cook for about 5 minutes, then stir in the soft cream cheese and stir until evenly mixed and the sauce is deep pink in colour.

Drain the cooked pasta thoroughly, then add to the vegetable mixture. Stir gently over a very low heat for 1 minute. Serve immediately.

ANNEMARIE PAPATHEOFILOU • SUMMERTOWN, OXFORDSHIRE

Rice & Grain Dishes

Mixed Rice
with Artichoke Hearts

Serves 4

This is equally good hot or cold. Either way, I like to serve it as a main course with a tangy sauce, such as a Hollandaise or Bearnaise, or even some good bought mayonnaise flavoured with extra lemon juice, together with a salad of crisp leaves, or some lightly cooked green beans and perhaps a tomato salad.

125 g (4 oz) brown rice
50 g (2 oz) wild rice
125 g (4 oz) white basmati rice
sea salt
4 globe artichokes
squeeze of lemon juice
30-45 ml (2-3 tbsp) chopped mixed herbs, ie parsley, tarragon,
chives, chervil, as available
freshly ground black pepper

Wash the brown rice and the wild rice by rinsing them together in a sieve under cold running water. Then put them into a saucepan with 450 ml (¾ pint) water and a good pinch of sea salt, and bring to the boil. Cover the pan, turn the heat down very low and leave the rice to cook for 40 minutes, when it should be tender, and all the water absorbed. If there's still some water left, put the lid back on the pan and leave it to stand, off the heat, for another 15 minutes.

Meanwhile wash the basmati rice in the same way. Half-fill a medium-large saucepan with water and bring to the boil, then add the rice and a good pinch of salt. Boil, uncovered, for about 10 minutes, or until the rice is just tender, then drain into a sieve and rinse with hot water. Drain and add to the brown rice mixture.

While the rice is cooking, prepare the artichoke hearts. Cut the leaves, stem and hairy choke from the artichokes, leaving just the bases. Squeeze a little lemon juice over the bases to preserve the colour. Put them into a saucepan, cover with water and simmer for about 15 minutes until just tender. Drain and slice or cut into quarters.

Add the cooked artichoke hearts to the rice mixture, together with the chopped herbs. Check the seasoning, and add salt, pepper and lemon juice to taste. Mix gently with a fork, to avoid mashing the rice.

If necessary this can be kept warm – or reheated – in a covered casserole in a preheated moderate oven at 180-200°C (350-400°F) mark 4-6.

ROSE ELLIOT

Millet with Spring Onions and Almonds

Serves 4

Millet is a health-giving grain which cooks to a pretty pale yellow colour and makes
a pleasant change from rice. It's good with a light spicing of cinnamon and cloves.
I like to serve this with a salad of grated carrot tossed in a mustardy
vinaigrette on a bed of crisp iceberg lettuce leaves.

15 ml (1 tbsp) olive oil
250 g (9 oz) millet
piece of cinnamon stick
4 cloves
1 bunch of spring onions, trimmed and chopped
50 g (2 oz) sultanas
sea salt and freshly ground black pepper
50 g (2 oz) flaked almonds

Heat the oil in a large saucepan and add the millet, then stir-fry over the heat
for a few minutes, until the millet has a toasted aroma and some of the grains
start to pop. Then, standing well back, pour in 600 ml (1 pint) of boiling water.
Add the cinnamon and cloves, cover and cook for 20 minutes.

Stir in the spring onions and sultanas. Check whether all the water has been
absorbed and, if not, cover the pan and leave it to stand, off the heat, for a
further 5 minutes or so. Check the seasoning and add the nuts. Stir the mixture
gently with a fork to fluff it, and serve.

ROSE ELLIOT

Marrow Rice

Serves 4

This is a nice easy summer dish which will cook itself while you're in the garden. If you serve it with grated cheese, or add some sunflower seeds or roasted cashew nuts at the end, you will have a protein-rich main dish.

1 small young vegetable marrow
60 ml (4 tbsp) oil
2 large onions, sliced
1 large green pepper, cored, seeded and sliced
225 g (8 oz) long-grain rice
2 garlic cloves, crushed
1 bay leaf
4 tomatoes, skinned
600 ml (1 pint) water
salt and freshly ground black pepper

TO GARNISH:
chopped parsley

Wash the marrow and cut it into cubes; the peel and the seeds will probably be tender enough to eat too.

Heat the oil in a large, heavy-based pan and fry the onions for 5 minutes, then add the marrow, green pepper, rice, garlic, bay leaf, tomatoes and water. Add salt and pepper to taste.

Bring to the boil, then turn the heat right down and put a lid on the pan. Cook very gently until the vegetables are tender, the rice is cooked and all the liquid is absorbed. Check the seasoning. Sprinkle with chopped parsley and serve immediately.

ROSE ELLIOT

Risotto Piedmontaise

Serves 2

*A traditional risotto from northern Italy, flavoured with mushrooms,
peas and Parmesan.*

50 g (2 oz) butter or margarine
175 g (6 oz) Italian Arborio rice
600 ml (1 pint) boiling vegetable stock or water
125 g (4 oz) mushrooms, finely sliced
125 g (4 oz) cooked peas
50 g (2 oz) Parmesan cheese, freshly grated
45 ml (3 tbsp) lemon juice
salt and freshly ground black pepper

Melt the butter or margarine in a heavy-based pan. Add the rice, turn to coat in
the butter and fry for a few minutes. Add a third of the stock and cook, stirring,
until all the liquid is absorbed. Add another third of the stock and cook,
stirring, until absorbed. Repeat with the remaining liquid. When all the liquid
is absorbed the rice should be cooked but still firm to the bite; this will take
about 20 minutes.

Stir in the mushrooms, cooked peas and grated cheese, and heat through,
stirring, for about 5 minutes. Add the lemon juice and salt and pepper to taste.
Serve immediately.

SIR JOHN GIELGUD

Rice with Sweet Pepper Relish

Serves 4

This simple vegetable and rice dish is popular in Malawi. Use a mixture of red, yellow and green peppers if you prefer.

5 green peppers
2 carrots
25 g (1 oz) butter
1 small onion, chopped
2 medium tomatoes, chopped
75 ml (5 tbsp) water
salt
225 g (8 oz) long-grain rice

Halve, core and seed the peppers, then cut into squares. Peel and finely dice the carrots. Melt the butter in a saucepan, add the onion and cook until softened. Add the tomatoes and simmer until softened. Add the green peppers and carrots and cook until softened. Add the water, cover and cook over moderate heat for 10 minutes. Season with salt to taste.

Meanwhile cook the rice in boiling salted water. Drain the rice if necessary and serve with the sweet pepper relish.

STELLA • MULANJE, MALAWI

Fragrant Saffron Pilau

Serves 6

A delicious accompaniment to Indian dishes, such as Spinach Dal (page 93), Green Beans with Cumin (page 56) and Aubergine and Yogurt Relish (page 57). If you are able to find them, morels add a distinctive flavour. You could alternatively use dried ones, soaked overnight; in this case use the liquid as part of the rice cooking water.

350 g (12 oz) basmati rice
60 ml (4 tbsp) oil
225 g (8 oz) button mushrooms or morels, sliced
3 cloves
6 green cardomom pods
1 stick cassia bark or cinnamon
600 ml (1 pint) water
2.5 ml (½ tsp) saffron strands
10 ml (2 tsp) caster sugar
salt and freshly ground black pepper

Wash the rice in several changes of cold water. Place in a bowl, add 1 litre (1¾ pints) cold water and leave to soak for 30 minutes. Drain.

Heat the oil in a large pan, add the mushrooms, cloves, cardomom pods, cassia bark or cinnamon, and rice. Cook, stirring, over moderate heat for 1-2 minutes.

Add the water, saffron, sugar and seasoning. Bring to the boil, stirring. Reduce the heat, cover tightly and cook very gently for about 15 minutes, or until all the liquid is absorbed and the rice is tender.

Adjust the seasoning and fluff up the rice with a fork before serving.

MOYRA FRASER • GOOD HOUSEKEEPING

Spinach
and Wild Rice Pilaf

Serves 4

A tasty oven baked pilaf, flavoured with spinach and thyme.

225 g (8 oz) wild rice
75 g (3 oz) butter
1 medium onion, diced
salt and freshly ground black pepper
600 ml (1 pint) stock
5 ml (1 tsp) chopped thyme leaves
1 bay leaf
225 g (8 oz) spinach, washed and shredded

Preheat the oven to 200°C (400°F) mark 6. Wash the wild rice in cold water; drain.

Heat 50 g (2 oz) butter in a heavy-based frying pan. Add the onion and cook until soft and translucent. Stir in the wild rice and season with salt and pepper. Add the chicken stock, thyme and bay leaf. Pour into a greased 2 litre (5 pint) casserole. Bake uncovered in the preheated oven for 50 minutes.

Place the shredded spinach in a large saucepan with the remaining butter. Season with salt and pepper. Cover and cook for 1 minute, then remove from the heat. Drain thoroughly. Remove the rice from the oven and discard the bay leaf. Fluff up with a fork and toss with the spinach. Serve immediately.

ABOVE: Easy Homemade Bread *(page 160)*
LEFT: Creamy Potato, Parsnip and Butter Bean Soup *(page 20)*
RIGHT: Asparagus Soup *(page 16)*; *BELOW*: Midweek Soup *(page 18)*

Above: Mushroom Roulade (page 116)
Below: Kingsmead Leek and Potato Puffs (page 103)

ABOVE: Apple and Fennel Salad (page 48)
BELOW: Roasted Pepper, Aubergine and Artichoke Salad (page 45)

Penne with Onion, Peppers and Aubergine (page 62)

Mixed Rice Salad with Nuts and Apricots

Serves 4

This delicious mixed basmati and wild rice salad is flavoured with a variety of nuts and seeds, dried apricots and coriander. It can be served warm or cold.

25 g (1 oz) butter
1 onion, sliced
3 garlic cloves, crushed
125 g (4 oz) blanched almonds
25 g (1 oz) pine nuts
25 g (1 oz) sunflower seeds
25 g (1 oz) pistachio nuts
15 g (½ oz) poppy seeds
50 g (2 oz) wild rice
300 g (10 oz) basmati rice
1.25 ml (¼ tsp) turmeric
50 g (2 oz) dried apricots, chopped
45 ml (3 tbsp) chopped coriander leaves

TO SERVE:
garlic and honey vinaigrette

Melt the butter in a pan, add the onion and garlic and fry, stirring, until softened. Add the almonds and pine nuts and fry gently, stirring frequently, for about 5 minutes until browned. Add the sunflower seeds, pistachio nuts and poppy seeds. Remove from the heat and set aside.

Bring a saucepan of salted water to the boil. Add the wild rice and cook for 10 minutes, then add half the basmati rice. Add the rest of the basmati rice to another pan of boiling salted water with the turmeric. Cover and cook for 10-15 minutes until the rice in each pan is al dente (just tender). Drain thoroughly.

Combine both types of rice in a large bowl. Add the fried nut mixture, apricots and coriander. Toss lightly to mix. Just before serving, mix in a little garlic and honey vinaigrette.

JUDY BUGG

Sweetcorn Fritters

Serves 4

Serve these tasty fritters as a snack, accompaniment, or with a crispy leaf salad as a light meal.

325 g (11 oz) can sweetcorn kernels, drained, or 3-4 fresh corn cobs
15 ml (1 tbsp) chopped parsley
1 egg
1 onion, chopped
salt
30 ml (2 tbsp) flour
a little milk
oil for deep-frying

If using fresh corn, cook in boiling water for about 10 minutes, then drain and cut the kernels from the cobs. Mix the sweetcorn, parsley, egg and onion together in a bowl. Add salt to taste. Stir in the flour a little at a time to thicken the mixture, adding milk to moisten as necessary.

Heat the oil in a deep-fat fryer until it is very hot. Drop spoonfuls of the mixture into the hot oil and deep-fry until light brown. Drain on absorbent kitchen paper. Repeat until all the mixture is used. Serve immediately.

Baked Corn

Serves 2

Serve this cheesy corn bake with a salad or green vegetable and crusty bread.

325 g (11 oz) can sweetcorn, drained, or 4 fresh corn cobs
2 eggs
15 g (½ oz) margarine
generous pinch of chilli powder
1 garlic clove, crushed or chopped
5 ml (1 tsp) flour
salt and freshly ground black pepper
125 g (4 oz) Gruyère or Cheddar cheese, thinly sliced

Preheat the oven to 170°C (325°F) mark 3. If using fresh corn, cut the kernels from the cobs. Beat the eggs lightly in a bowl, then add the sweetcorn.

Melt the margarine in a saucepan and stir in the chilli powder, garlic and flour. Cook, stirring, for 1 minute, then remove from the heat and combine with the corn and egg mixture. Add seasoning.

Pour half of the mixture into a well oiled 900 ml (1½ pint) casserole dish. Cover with a layer of cheese slices. Spread the remaining corn mixture over this layer and top with the remaining cheese slices.

Bake in the preheated oven for about 45 minutes until golden and bubbling. Serve immediately.

Hot Black Bean and Rice Salad with Pomegranates

Serves 4-6

I always use fruits in season and pomegranates – sadly neglected by some – are one of my favourites. Their jewel-like seeds make wonderful garnishes, and they are a superb addition to salads. I am particularly keen on this recipe which is colourful, tasty and relatively cheap to prepare. It can be served as a meal in itself or as an accompaniment to cold pies and quiches or hot nut roasts.

125 g (4 oz) dried black kidney beans, soaked overnight
225 g (8 oz) long-grain brown rice
salt and freshly ground black pepper
2 pomegranates
1 large red pepper
1 large green pepper
60 ml (4 tbsp) olive oil
1 large onion, thinly sliced
1 garlic clove, chopped
5 ml (1 tsp) paprika
5 ml (1 tsp) ground coriander
juice of ½ lemon

Drain the black beans, rinse thoroughly, then place in a saucepan and add double the volume of water. Bring to the boil and boil vigorously for 10 minutes, then lower the heat, cover and simmer for about 1-1½ hours until tender. Drain.

Meanwhile, cook the rice in lightly salted boiling water for 40 minutes, or until just tender. Drain, rinse under cold running water and then drain again.

Halve the pomegranates and scoop out the seeds, reserving as much juice as possible. Halve, core and seed the peppers, then cut into thin strips.

Heat the oil in a large frying pan over a high heat. Add the red pepper and stir-fry for 2 minutes. Remove from the pan with a slotted spoon; keep warm.

Add the green pepper, onion and garlic to the pan and stir-fry for 2 minutes. Stir in the spices, then the rice, beans and pomegranate seeds and juice. Heat through, stirring. Add the lemon juice and mix well. Check the seasoning.

Transfer the salad to a serving plate and surround with the strips of red pepper. Serve immediately.

GAIL DUFF

Bean & Lentil Dishes

Provençal Bean Casserole

Serves 4

This easy-to-make casserole is good with rice, pasta or baked potatoes, but I like it best with some crunchy garlic bread and a simple mixed salad. If there's any over, it can be reheated, and often tastes extra good the second time, as well as being good cold, as a starter or salad.

1 large aubergine, diced
sea salt
2 red peppers
30 ml (2 tbsp) olive oil
1 onion, sliced
2 garlic cloves, crushed
700 g (1½ lb) courgettes, sliced
225 g (8 oz) button mushrooms, sliced
425 g (15 oz) can tomatoes
425 g (15 oz) can flageolet beans, drained
freshly ground black pepper

Put the aubergine into a colander, sprinkle with salt and leave for about 30 minutes to degorge. If you dislike the outer skin of the peppers, peel with a potato peeler – you needn't take every scrap off. Halve, core and deseed the peppers, then slice.

Heat the oil in a large saucepan, add the onion and cook, covered, without browning, for 5 minutes. Rinse the aubergine under cold water and pat dry. Add to the onion, with the garlic and peppers, and cook for a further 10 minutes. Add the courgettes, mushrooms and tomatoes, with their juice and cook for a further 15 minutes, or until all the vegetables are tender. Add the flageolet beans and heat through. Season with salt and pepper before serving.

Rose Elliot

Cannellini Beans with Red Peppers and Olives

Serves 2

One of those vegetarian dishes which you can throw together really quickly. It can be served as a first course or as part of a main course, with good bread and a leafy salad featuring rocket perhaps, or fresh basil, and some sliced avocado. Alternatively serve with some canned stuffed vine leaves, lemon wedges and a dollop of good houmus, and bread, of course.

2 red peppers
425 g (15 oz) can cannellini beans, drained
10 black olives
squeeze of lemon juice
15-30 ml (1-2 tbsp) olive oil
sea salt and freshly ground black pepper

Cut the peppers into quarters and lay them, skin-side uppermost, on a grill pan. Put them under a very hot grill for about 15 minutes, or until the skin has blackened and blistered – move them around during this time if necessary to ensure that they grill evenly. Then put the pieces into a bowl and cover. Leave until cool enough to handle, then remove the skin with a sharp knife – it should come off quite easily. Discard the seeds. Rinse the pepper pieces, slice into strips, and put them into a shallow casserole.

Add the cannellini beans to the peppers, along with the olives, lemon juice, olive oil, and salt and pepper to taste. Mix well, and if there's time, leave for an hour or so to allow the flavours to blend.

I prefer to serve this dish at room temperature but it can be covered and warmed through in a moderate oven for 15 minutes or so.

ROSE ELLIOT

Beans Granados

Serves 8

This kidney bean, corn and squash casserole comes from Chile. Instead of fresh corn-on-the-cob you could use two 300 g (10 oz) cans of sweetcorn for convenience.

500 g (1 lb 2 oz) dried red kidney beans, soaked overnight
50 g (2 oz) butter
2 onions, finely chopped
6 corn cobs
250 g (9 oz) squash, peeled and cubed
500 ml (16 fl oz) vegetable stock or milk
salt and freshly ground black pepper to taste

Drain the kidney beans and place in a saucepan with double their volume of water. Bring to the boil and boil steadily for 10 minutes, then lower the heat, cover and simmer for about 45 minutes until tender. Drain well.

Melt the butter in a pan, add the onions and fry gently until golden brown. Meanwhile if using fresh corn, cut the kernels from the cobs. Add the sweetcorn kernels to the onions with the squash. Fry until softened, stirring frequently.

Add the kidney beans and stock or milk. Season with salt and pepper to taste. Cover and simmer gently for about 20 minutes. Serve hot.

Creamed Beans and Sweet Potatoes

Serves 6

400 g (14 oz) dried black-eyed beans, soaked overnight
700 g (1½ lb) sweet potato, peeled and cut into chunks
50 g (2 oz) butter
salt
4 tomatoes, sliced

Drain the black-eyed beans and place in a saucepan with double their volume of water. Bring to the boil, lower the heat, cover and simmer for about 25 minutes until half-cooked. Add the sweet potatoes to the pan and continue cooking until both the beans and potatoes are soft, about 20 minutes. Drain, then mash with the butter and salt to taste until smooth. Serve garnished with tomato slices.

Haricot Bean Salad

Serves 4

Serve this simple yet delicious Turkish salad with pitta bread or good crusty bread.

125 g (4 oz) dried haricot beans, soaked overnight
60 ml (4 tbsp) olive oil
juice of ½ lemon, or to taste
salt and freshly ground black pepper
2 hard-boiled eggs
4 black olives, halved and stoned
1 tomato, thinly sliced

Drain the haricot beans and place in a saucepan with double their volume of water. Bring to the boil, lower the heat, cover and simmer for about 1 hour until soft and tender, but still retaining their shape. Drain thoroughly and transfer to a bowl.

While the haricot beans are still hot, add the olive oil, lemon juice, salt and pepper to taste and toss to mix.

Cut each hard-boiled egg into 8 wedges and add to the salad with the olives and tomato slices. Toss lightly, taking care to avoid crumbling the eggs.

CLAUDIA RODEN

Kirsty's Chilli

Serves 2

This must be the easiest veggie recipe in the world! It is popular with my vegetarian daughter, and goes well with brown bread or rice.

15 ml (1 tbsp) oil
1 onion, chopped
1 garlic clove, crushed
1 red, green or yellow pepper, cored, seeded and chopped
1-2 tomatoes, finely chopped
425 g (15 oz) can red kidney beans, drained
5 ml (1 tsp) dried oregano or marjoram
5 ml (1 tsp) chilli powder
salt and freshly ground black pepper

Heat the oil in a large saucepan, add the onion and cook until softened, then add the garlic and cook gently for 1 minute. Add the remaining ingredients, stir well, cover and cook for 20 minutes.

Serve with rice or brown bread.

IAN MCCASKILL

Homemade Baked Beans

Serves 4-6

Served with brown rice this dish is beautifully balanced nutritionally. I also like to eat it with jacket potatoes and coleslaw. If you use precooked beans you will need 700 g (1½ lb) cooked weight.

350 g (12 oz) dried black-eyed beans, soaked overnight
15 ml (1 tbsp) olive oil
1 medium onion, chopped
3 garlic cloves, crushed
5 ml (1 tsp) cumin seeds
5 ml (1 tsp) ground coriander
1 large apple, peeled, cored and grated
1 large carrot, peeled and grated
1½ x 425 g (15 oz) cans tomatoes
15 ml (1 tbsp) black molasses
10 ml (2 tsp) cider vinegar
15 ml (1 tbsp) tomato purée
150 ml (¼ pint) water
salt and freshly ground black pepper

Drain the black-eyed beans, rinse well and put into a saucepan with double their volume of water. Bring to the boil and boil steadily for 10 minutes, then lower the heat, cover and simmer for about 30 minutes until slightly softened. Drain.

Preheat the oven to 200°C (400°F) mark 6. Heat the oil in a large flameproof casserole and add the onion, garlic, cumin and coriander. Cook, stirring occasionally, until the onion is softened. Add the grated apple and carrot and fry gently for 3 minutes.

Add the black-eyed beans, tomatoes, molasses, vinegar, tomato purée and water. Add seasoning to taste and stir well. Cover with a tight-fitting lid and bake in the preheated oven for about 40 minutes.

C. MOORE • BELFAST

Channa Dal

Serves 3

This hot, spicy chick pea dal is dry, rather than thin and soup-like. If you cannot obtain fresh coconut, use unsweetened desiccated coconut – but only as a last resort!

225 g (8 oz) chick peas, soaked overnight
1 onion, finely chopped
50 g (2 oz) ghee, butter or margarine
2.5 ml (½ tsp) turmeric
5 ml (1 tsp) cumin seeds
5 ml (1 tsp) mustard seeds
30 ml (2 tbsp) freshly grated coconut
salt
2 green chillies, chopped

TO GARNISH:
chopped coriander leaves

Put the chick peas in a large saucepan with about 1.2 litres (2 pints) water and bring to the boil. Lower the heat, cover and simmer for 1½ hours or until tender. Drain.

Heat the fat in a heavy-based pan, add the onion and cook until softened and pale golden in colour. Add the turmeric, cumin and mustard seeds and cook until the mustard seeds begin to splutter and burst.

Add the chick peas and fry, turning, for a few minutes. Lower the heat, cover and cook gently for 10 minutes. Stir in the coconut, chillies and salt to taste. Cover and cook for 5 minutes. Serve sprinkled with chopped coriander leaves.

Spinach Dal

Serves 6

This is delicious served with Fragrant Saffron Pilau (page 79), Green Beans with Cumin (page 56), and Aubergine and Yogurt Relish (page 57). If you prefer a milder flavour, halve the quantity of chilli powder or omit it altogether. Use split moong dal available from Indian shops or red or green lentils.

225 g (8 oz) moong dal or lentils
450 g (1 lb) frozen leaf spinach, thawed
75 g (3 oz) ghee or butter
1 onion, finely chopped
1 garlic clove, crushed
5 ml (1 tsp) ground coriander
5 ml (1 tsp) turmeric
5 ml (1 tsp) chilli powder
300 ml (½ pint) water
salt and freshly ground black pepper

Wash the moong dal or lentils, then soak in cold water for 2 hours; drain well. Drain and chop the spinach.

Heat the ghee or butter in a large sauté pan. Add the onion and garlic and cook, stirring for 2-3 minutes. Stir in the spices and dal. Cook, stirring, for 1-2 minutes. Add the water and seasoning. Bring to the boil, cover and simmer for about 15 minutes or until the dal is almost tender, adding a little more water if necessary.

Stir in the spinach and cook over a high heat, stirring, for 4-5 minutes or until thoroughly hot and all excess moisture has been driven off. Adjust the seasoning before serving.

MOYRA FRASER • GOOD HOUSEKEEPING

Cheese and Lentil Loaf

Serves 4

This tasty loaf can be eaten hot or cold, with watercress or other green salad. I developed the recipe for my daughter, Sheila, who announced she was a vegetarian on her return from a holiday in Australia! As a variation, you can bake a layer of sliced tomatoes in the middle of the loaf.

175 g (6 oz) red or green lentils, soaked overnight and drained
350 ml (12 fl oz) water
125 g (4 oz) Cheddar cheese, grated
1 onion, finely chopped
juice of 1 lemon
15 ml (1 tbsp) chopped parsley
1 egg, beaten
45 ml (3 tbsp) cream
salt and freshly ground black pepper

Preheat the oven to 180°C (350°F) mark 4. Rinse the lentils thoroughly then put them in a saucepan with the water and bring to the boil. Lower the heat, cover and cook for 20 minutes if using red lentils; 30 minutes for green ones; until the water is absorbed; check after 10 minutes, adding a little more water if necessary to moisten. Season with salt and pepper to taste.

Add the cheese, onion, lemon juice and parsley to the stiff lentil 'purée'. Mix the beaten egg with the cream and stir into the lentil mixture.

Turn into a well buttered 450 g (1 lb) loaf tin and press the mixture down firmly. Bake in the preheated oven for 45-50 minutes until the top is browned and the loaf is firm to the touch. Serve hot or cold, cut into slices.

MRS AUDREY ADDISON • LYMM, CHESHIRE

Savoury
Pastry Dishes

Oyster Mushroom and Pine Nut Tartlets

Serves 4

These little tartlets can be served as a first course, although I think they make an excellent light main course, served with baby new potatoes and a mixed leaf salad.

FOR THE PASTRY:
50 g (2 oz) plain flour
50 g (2 oz) plain wholewheat flour
pinch of salt
50 g (2 oz) butter
1 egg yolk

FOR THE FILLING:
1 whole bulb of garlic, unpeeled
30 ml (2 tbsp) single cream
freshly ground black pepper
25 g (1 oz) butter
30 ml (2 tbsp) olive oil
350-450 g (12 oz-1 lb) oyster mushrooms, sliced
50 g (2 oz) pine nuts

Preheat the oven to 200°C (400°F) mark 6 and put a large baking sheet in the oven to heat up. Sift the flours into a bowl or food processor with a pinch of salt, adding any bran left in the sieve, too. Rub in the butter, or process, with the feeder tube removed, until the mixture looks like fine breadcrumbs. Add the egg yolk and bind to a dough, adding a few drops of cold water if necessary.

Divide the dough into four. Roll each piece out as thinly as possible and use to line 4 individual 10 cm (4 inch) loose-bottomed flan tins. Trim edges and prick the bases. Put the tartlet tins onto the hot baking sheet and bake in the oven for about 15 minutes, or until the pastry is set and very lightly browned.

To make the filling, boil the garlic in water to cover for about 15 minutes until tender. Drain and cool, then pop the garlic cloves out of their skins and mash with the cream to a purée. Season. Heat the butter and oil in a pan and fry the mushrooms for 5 minutes, or until tender. Add salt and pepper to taste.

To finish the tartlets, remove them from their tins and place on a baking sheet. Divide the garlic purée between them, top with oyster mushrooms and sprinkle with pine nuts. Bake in the oven for about 15 minutes until they are heated through, and the pine nuts are lightly browned.

ROSE ELLIOT

Asparagus and Goat's Cheese Strudel

Serves 4

Served with lightly-cooked early vegetables, this makes a good vegetarian main course for a summer meal. A creamy herb sauce – made by stirring chopped fresh herbs, especially chives, tarragon and parsley, into soured cream, crème fraîche or thick creamy yogurt – is the perfect complement.

400 g (14 oz) potatoes
250 g (9 oz) asparagus
150 g (5 oz) soft white goat's cheese
30-45 ml (2-3 tbsp) chopped chervil or parsley
sea salt and freshly ground black pepper
1 packet filo pastry
50 g (2 oz) butter, melted

Preheat the oven to 200°C (400°F) mark 6. Peel the potatoes and cut them into 1 cm (½ inch) dice: trim the asparagus, removing any tough stem ends. Cut the asparagus into 1 cm (½ inch) pieces, keeping the tips separate from the stems. Put the potatoes into a saucepan, add cold water to just cover and bring to the boil. Boil for about 5 minutes, or until almost tender, then add the asparagus stems and cook for a further 2-3 minutes. Add the asparagus tips and cook for about 3 minutes until all the vegetables are just tender. Drain, leave to cool a little, then stir in the goat's cheese and season with salt and pepper.

Spread out two sheets of filo pastry, side by side and slightly overlapping, to make one large sheet about 30 cm (12 inches) square, or a little larger. Brush this all over with melted butter, then put two more sheets on top, and brush again with butter. Repeat with two more filo sheets and brush with butter so that you have a layer of three double sheets. Now spread the asparagus mixture on top, leaving the edges clear. Fold the edges over the filling, then roll the strudel up lightly.

Transfer the strudel to a baking sheet, and brush it all over with butter. Bake the strudel for 20-30 minutes, or until it is golden brown and crisp. Serve immediately.

ROSE ELLIOT

Onion Flan

Serves 4

This is a lovely flan with a very thin, crisp case and light, savoury filling. It is good cold, as well as hot, and the pastry keeps its crispness. Of course it's nicest made with the double cream but I have given two alternatives.

FOR THE PASTRY:
50 g (2 oz) plain wholewheat flour
50 g (2 oz) plain white flour
pinch of salt
50 g (2 oz) butter
1 egg yolk
a little chilled water to mix, if necessary

FOR THE FILLING:
50 g (2 oz) butter
350 g (12 oz) onion, chopped
150 ml (¼ pint) double cream, soured cream or yogurt
2 egg yolks
salt and freshly ground black pepper
freshly grated nutmeg

Preheat the oven to 200°C (400°F) mark 6. To make the pastry, sift the flours into a bowl with the salt, adding any bran left in the sieve too. Rub in the butter until the mixture looks like fine breadcrumbs, then mix in the egg yolk and a very small amount of cold water, if necessary to make a smooth dough. Alternatively you can make the pastry in a food processor.

Roll out the dough thinly on a lightly floured surface and use to line a 23 cm (9 inch) flan tin or pie dish. Leave to rest in a cool place for an hour or so. Prick the bottom of the pastry case lightly, cover with a piece of greaseproof paper and some baking beans and bake blind in the preheated oven for 15 minutes – it helps to stand the flan dish on a heated baking sheet as this conducts the heat well and cooks the bottom of the flan crisply. Remove the beans and paper and return the flan to the oven for 4-5 minutes to finish cooking the bottom; remove from the oven and cool. Lower the oven temperature to 180°C (350°F) mark 4.

While the flan is cooking, make the filling. Melt the butter in a pan, add the onion and fry lightly until softened, about 10 minutes, then remove from the heat. Allow to cool slightly, then add the cream or yogurt, the egg yolks and a good seasoning of salt, pepper and nutmeg. Spread the mixture evenly in the flan case and bake in the oven for about 30 minutes, until it is set.

ROSE ELLIOT

Sweetcorn Soufflé Flan

Serves 4

23 cm (9 inch) flan case

FOR THE FILLING:
25 g (1 oz) butter
30 ml (2 tbsp) flour
300 ml (½ pint) hot milk
225 g (8 oz) cooked sweetcorn kernels
2 eggs, separated
salt and freshly ground black pepper
25-50 g (1-2 oz) cheese, grated

Peheat the oven, make the flan case and bake blind, as described opposite.

To make the filling, melt the butter in a small pan, add the flour and cook for 1 minute. Remove from the heat and whisk in the milk. Cook, whisking until thickened. Cool slightly, then add the sweetcorn, egg yolks and seasoning.

In a separate bowl, whisk the egg whites stiffly, then, fold into the sweetcorn mixture. Spoon into the flan case and scatter with grated cheese. Stand the flan dish on a baking tray in the oven and bake at 190°C (375°F) mark 5 for about 25 minutes, until risen and golden. Serve immediately.

ROSE ELLIOT

Cheese and Onion Flan

Serves 4

about 125 g (4 oz) homemade shortcrust pastry (flour weight)
125 g (4 oz) Cheddar cheese, grated
1 Spanish onion, sliced into rings
45 ml (3 tbsp) 'top of the milk'
salt and freshly ground black pepper

Preheat the oven to 180°C (350°F) mark 4. Roll out the pastry on a lightly floured surface and use about three quarters to line an 18 cm (7 inch) flan tin or dish. Sprinkle with the cheese, then arrange the onion rings on top. Re-roll the pastry trimmings and cut into strips. Arrange these in a lattice over the filling. Sprinkle with the milk and seasoning. Bake in the oven for 30 minutes.

DORA BRYAN

Spinach Quiche

Serves 6-8

This is an adaptation of one of my mother's recipes. I like to serve it with a salad and spinach tagliatelle or rice.

FOR THE PASTRY:
350 g (12 oz) wholemeal flour
5 ml (1 tsp) salt
200 ml (⅓ pint) sunflower oil
75 ml (5 tbsp) water

FOR THE FILLING:
6 eggs, size 3
about 200 ml (⅓ pint) milk
salt and freshly ground black pepper
270 g (10 oz) can chopped spinach, well drained

TO GARNISH (OPTIONAL):
tomato slices
snipped chives

Preheat the oven to 170°C (325°F) mark 3. Sift the flour and salt into a bowl and make a well in the centre. Beat the oil with the water, then pour into the well and stir into the flour to form a dough. Roll out the dough on a lightly floured surface and use to line a well oiled 25 cm (10 inch) flan tin or dish. Leave to rest in a cool place.

Beat the eggs thoroughly in a measuring jug, then add an equal volume of milk and seasoning to taste. Stir in the spinach, then pour the mixture into the pastry case. Bake in the oven for about 40 minutes until the filling is firm and golden brown. Garnish with tomato slices and/or snipped chives if you wish.

RECA MACLEOD • TEWKESBURY, GLOUCESTERSHIRE

Leek and Mustard Quiche

Serves 4-6

*I invented this recipe to combine two of my favourites – leeks and cheese
sauce flavoured with grainy mustard. It goes well with jacket potatoes and
a watercress garnish.*

FOR THE PASTRY:
225 g (8 oz) wholemeal 'granary' self-raising flour
110 g (4 oz) margarine, in pieces
chilled water to mix

FOR THE FILLING:
4 medium leeks, cleaned
15 ml (1 tbsp) wholegrain mustard
125 g (4 oz) Cheddar cheese, grated
1 egg
150 ml (¼ pint) milk
pinch of salt

Preheat the oven to 220°C (425°F) mark 7. To make the pastry, put the flour
into a mixing bowl and rub in the margarine until the mixture resembles fine
breadcrumbs. Add a little water and mix to a smooth dough. Alternatively,
make the pastry in a food processor.

Roll out the pastry on a lightly floured surface and use to line a 25 cm
(10 inch) flan tin. Line with a sheet of greaseproof paper and baking beans and
bake blind in the preheated oven for 15 minutes. Remove the paper and beans.
Lower the oven temperature to 200°C (400°F) mark 6.

Cut the leeks into 2.5 cm (1 inch) pieces and steam for 10 minutes, or cook
in a little boiling water until tender. Spread the mustard over the base of the
flan case, then place the leeks on top of the mustard. Sprinkle evenly with the
grated cheese.

In a bowl whisk the egg with the milk and salt, then pour over the cheese.
Bake near the top of the oven for 40 minutes until lightly browned on top.

MURIEL RICHARDS • ST. DENYS, HAMPSHIRE

Righteous Lentil Flan

Serves 4-6

*This is delicious, hot or cold, served with baked potatoes, a green salad and
sliced tomatoes.*

FOR THE PASTRY:

175 g (6 oz) plain wholemeal flour
125 g (4 oz) margarine
25 g (1 oz) rolled oats
15 g (½ oz) sesame seeds
15 g (½ oz) nuts, finely chopped
30-45 ml (2-3 tbsp) chilled water

FOR THE FILLING:

125 g (4 oz) Continental brown lentils
30 ml (2 tbsp) chopped mixed herbs
30 ml (2 tbsp) oil
1 large onion, finely chopped
2 garlic cloves, finely chopped
30 ml (2 tbsp) soy sauce
30 ml (2 tbsp) tomato purée
1.25 ml (¼ tsp) freshly grated nutmeg
2 eggs, beaten
75 g (3 oz) Cheddar cheese, grated
freshly ground black pepper

To make the pastry, put the flour into a mixing bowl and rub in the margarine
until the mixture resembles fine breadcrumbs. Stir in the oats, sesame seeds
and chopped nuts. Mix in sufficient water to bind the mixture to a smooth
dough. Roll out the pastry on a lightly floured surface and use to line a 23 cm
(9 inch) flan tin or dish. Cover and leave to rest in a cool place.

For the filling, put the lentils in a saucepan with three times their volume of
water. Bring to the boil then lower the heat, cover and simmer for 20-30
minutes until tender. Drain and mix with 15 ml (1 tbsp) mixed herbs.

Preheat the oven to 190°C (375°F) mark 5. Heat the oil in a small pan, add
the onion and garlic and cook gently until softened. Add the soy sauce, tomato
purée, nutmeg and remaining mixed herbs. Cook gently for a few minutes. Add
to the beaten eggs with the lentils and cheese. Season with pepper to taste and
mix thoroughly.

Spread the filling in the pastry case and bake in the preheated oven for
35-40 minutes until the top is firm and lightly browned.

DOREEN GATHERCOLE • BLACKBURN, LANCASHIRE

Kingsmead Leek and Potato Puffs

Serves 6

This is a home-invented recipe which our family favours for Saturday lunch, with a salad.

300 ml (½ pint) Elmleigh vegetable cream
½ vegetable stock cube
50 g (2 oz) tarragon, finely chopped
700 g (1½ lb) potatoes
700 g (1½ lb) leeks, washed and sliced
30 ml (2 tbsp) vegetable oil
salt and freshly ground black pepper
6 sheets filo pastry
melted vegetable margarine for brushing

Preheat the oven to 180°C (350°F) mark 4. Put the vegetable cream in a saucepan, crumble in the stock cube and heat gently until dissolved. Add the freshly chopped tarragon and cook over a moderate heat for 1 minute. Transfer to a bowl and set aside.

Boil the potatoes until just tender; drain and cut into cubes. Sauté the leeks in the oil until just cooked. Add the potatoes and leeks to the tarragon cream sauce and mix together so that all the ingredients are coated in sauce. Season with salt and pepper to taste.

Lay the filo pastry sheets out on a large baking sheet, overlapping them to form a large cross. Alternatively cut each sheet in half to form two strips and overlap these to form individual crosses. Place the filling in the centre of the cross(es). Wrap the filo around the filling to enclose, and brush each parcel with melted vegetable margarine. Bake in the preheated oven allowing 25 minutes for the large parcel, 10-15 minutes for individual ones. Serve immediately.

DAVID PUTTNAM

Vegetable Samosas

Serves 4-6

FOR THE PASTRY:
175 g (6 oz) plain flour
2.5 ml (½ tsp) baking powder
5 ml (1 tsp) salt
40 g (1½ oz) white vegetable fat
a little chilled water to mix

FOR THE FILLING:
225 g (8 oz) potatoes
5 ml (1 tsp) paprika
5 ml (1 tsp) cumin seeds
5 ml (1 tsp) turmeric
5 ml (1 tsp) ground coriander
50 g (2 oz) peas, cooked
30 ml (2 tbsp) oil
1 onion, finely chopped
1 small bunch coriander leaves, chopped

TO COOK:
oil for deep-frying

To make the pastry, sift the flour with the baking powder and salt into a bowl. Rub in the white fat until the mixture resembles fine breadcrumbs. Add sufficient water to mix to a smooth dough. Set aside.

To make the filling, boil the potatoes in their skins until soft, then drain, peel and cut into pieces. Sprinkle with the spices and mix with the peas. Heat the oil in a pan, add the onion and fry until softened. Add the spiced potato mixture and fry briefly, stirring constantly, to cook the spices. Stir in the chopped coriander.

Shape the dough into balls, then cut each one in half. Make a hollow in each half and put some of the spiced potato mixture in each hollow. Sandwich the halves together and roll into balls.

Heat the oil in a deep-fat fryer. When it is very hot, deep-fry the balls in batches until crisp and brown. Drain on absorbent kitchen paper and serve.

INDIAN EMBASSY

Spring Rolls

Serves 5

These Vietnamese spring rolls are easy to make. You can buy spring roll wrappers from oriental food stores.

2 or 3 small packets cellophane noodles
3 large carrots, coarsely grated
2.5 ml (½ tsp) finely chopped fresh root ginger
10 ml (2 tsp) finely chopped garlic
2.5 ml (½ tsp) freshly ground black pepper
30 ml (2 tbsp) soy sauce
1 packet spring roll wrappers
a little milk for brushing
oil for deep-frying

Cook the noodles in boiling water for 4 minutes, then drain and cut into short lengths. Mix the noodles with the carrots, ginger, garlic, pepper and soy sauce.

Lay the spring roll wrappers out on a work surface and spread about 30 ml (2 tbsp) filling diagonally across the middle of each wrapper. Brush the edges with milk and fold in the sides, then roll up, making sure the parcels are well sealed with the milk.

Heat the oil in a deep-fat fryer. When it is really hot, deep-fry the spring rolls until crisp and golden. Drain on absorbent kitchen paper, then serve.

Greek Spinach Pie

Serves 4-6

This flaky, mouthwatering combination of spinach, cheese and filo pastry is popular throughout Greece where it is known as 'spanokopita'.

450 g (1 lb) spinach leaves, or 300 g (10 oz) packet frozen spinach, thawed
125 g (4 oz) feta, Gruyère or Cheddar cheese
225 g (8 oz) cottage cheese
3 eggs, beaten
1 onion, grated
30 ml (2 tbsp) chopped parsley
10 ml (2 tsp) chopped dill
2.5 ml (½ tsp) dried oregano
2.5 ml (½ tsp) salt
large pinch of freshly grated nutmeg
125 g (4 oz) margarine or butter, melted
12 sheets filo pastry

Preheat the oven to 180°C (350°F) mark 4. If using fresh spinach cook in a covered pan, with just the water clinging to the leaves after washing, for about 3 minutes. Chop the spinach and place in a bowl. Grate or crumble the feta, Gruyère or Cheddar cheese and add to the bowl. Stir in the cottage cheese, eggs, onion, herbs, salt and nutmeg until evenly mixed.

Grease a shallow rectangular baking dish or tin, about 30 x 12 cm (12 x 7 inches), with a little melted margarine or butter. Cut each filo pastry sheet in half and keep them covered with a damp tea towel as you work to prevent them drying out.

Line the base of the tin with a half-sheet of filo, folding the edges over as necessary to fit. Brush lightly with melted margarine. Layer a further 11 half-sheets on top, brushing each one with margarine.

Cover with the spinach mixture then layer the rest of the filo half-sheets on top, brushing each one with margarine and tucking in the sides. Cover the tin and bake in the preheated oven for 25 minutes, then uncover and bake for a further 5-10 minutes until golden brown. Let stand for 10 minutes. Cut into squares to serve.

Main
Vegetable
Dishes

Super Stir-Fry

Serves 2-3

*This is one of my favourite quick meals, put together from whatever
selection of interesting vegetables I can get at my local supermarket at the
end of a busy day.*

1 bunch of spring onions
150 g (5 oz) baby sweetcorn
150 g (5 oz) mangetout
225 g (8 oz) broccoli
150 g (5 oz) oyster mushrooms or shitake mushrooms
225 g (8 oz) carrots
30 ml (2 tbsp) olive oil
125 g (4 oz) roasted cashew nuts
salt and freshly ground black pepper

Trim and prepare all the vegetables as necessary, then cut them into bite-size
chunks. Just before you want to serve the stir-fry, heat the oil in a wok or large
saucepan. Add the carrots and stir-fry for about 4 minutes, then add the
broccoli and mushrooms and stir-fry for a further 4 minutes. Add the remaining
vegetables and cashew nuts. Continue to stir-fry for 2-3 minutes, until the
vegetables are all heated through but still crisp. Season – sparingly with salt if
the cashew nuts are salted. Serve at once.

ROSE ELLIOT

Courgette and Tomato Gratin

Serves 2-3

This is a slightly adapted version of Elizabeth David's recipe for Baked Courgettes and Tomatoes, which I think makes an excellent vegetarian main course with buttered baby vegetables or creamed spinach. It's one of my favourite vegetable dishes and I agree with Elizabeth David that two people can easily consume the whole lot! This quantity might serve 3 less greedy people, though, depending on how many vegetables you serve with it.

1 kg (2 lb) courgettes
sea salt
75 g (3 oz) butter
1 small garlic clove, crushed
30 ml (2 tbsp) chopped parsley
500 g (1 lb) tomatoes, skinned and chopped
freshly ground black pepper
50 g (2 oz) finely grated Parmesan cheese, or fine fresh white breadcrumbs,
slightly dried

Trim the courgettes and remove strips of peel along each one, using a vegetable peeler or canelle knife, leaving alternate strips unpeeled. Cut them into rounds about 5 mm (¼ inch) thick, then put into a colander, sprinkle with sea salt, and leave on one side to drain.

Preheat the oven to 220°C (425°F) mark 7. Melt 15 g (½ oz) of the butter in a saucepan and add the garlic, parsley, tomatoes, and a seasoning of salt and pepper. Let the tomatoes cook gently for about 15 minutes, until they are reduced to a thick purée, but not too dry. Remove from the heat and leave on one side while you prepare the courgettes.

Rinse the courgettes and pat them dry in a tea towel. Melt 25 g (1 oz) of the butter in a large saucepan or frying pan, add half of the courgette slices and fry gently until they are tender and look transparent; do not allow to brown. Remove and set aside. Melt another 25 g (1 oz) butter in the pan and fry the rest of the courgettes in the same way. Then gently mix all of the courgettes with the tomato sauce. Check the seasoning and add pepper and salt if necessary.

Spoon the mixture into a shallow casserole dish and smooth the top. Sprinkle with Parmesan or breadcrumbs and dot with the remaining 15 g (½ oz) butter. Bake in the oven for 25-30 minutes, until golden brown and bubbling.

ROSE ELLIOT

Courgette and Cheese Bake

Serves 2

I originally developed this recipe to use up a glut of plum tomatoes and courgettes. Though the flavour is good with canned tomatoes, you can of course use sliced fresh ones instead. I like to serve this with garlic or herb bread to soak up the juices.

30 ml (2 tbsp) sunflower oil
1 large onion, finely chopped
2 garlic cloves, finely chopped
2 medium courgettes, sliced
salt and freshly ground black pepper
425 g (15 oz) can chopped tomatoes
125 g (4 oz) Cheddar cheese, sliced
30 ml (2 tbsp) sunflower or sesame seeds

Preheat the oven to 180°C (350°F) mark 4. Heat the oil in a frying pan, add the onion and garlic and fry gently for 5 minutes. Add the courgette slices and fry for 5 minutes. Season with salt and pepper.

Transfer the courgette mixture to a greased ovenproof dish. Cover with the tomatoes, first draining these if there is a lot of juice. Arrange the cheese slices over the tomatoes and sprinkle with the sunflower or sesame seeds. Bake in the preheated oven for 30-40 minutes; if the dish appears to be browning too quickly, cover with foil. Serve hot.

KATE JOHNSON • FRODSHAM, CHESHIRE

Vegetarian Winter Savoury

Serves 4

I usually serve this with pasta or jacket potatoes. If preferred you can omit the cheese topping – the dish is very tasty without it!

25 g (1 oz) margarine or 30 ml (2 tbsp) oil
1 large onion, chopped
3 celery sticks, chopped
3 medium carrots, chopped
50 g (2 oz) mushrooms, chopped
425 g (15 oz) can chopped tomatoes
vegetable stock or water (see method)
50 g (2 oz) lentils
5 ml (1 tsp) yeast extract
5 ml (1 tsp) dried mixed herbs
salt and freshly ground black pepper
75 g (3 oz) Cheddar cheese, grated

Heat the margarine or oil in a large saucepan, add the onion, celery, carrots and mushrooms and fry gently for 10 minutes, stirring from time to time.

Meanwhile, drain the liquid from the tomatoes into a measuring jug and make up to 300 ml (½ pint) with vegetable stock or water. Add this liquid to the vegetable mixture and bring to the boil.

Add the lentils, cover and simmer for 20 minutes or until the lentils are soft and the vegetables are almost cooked. Add the tomatoes, together with the yeast extract, herbs and salt and pepper to taste.

Transfer the mixture to a large gratin dish and cover with the grated cheese. Place under a preheated hot grill until the cheese is golden brown and bubbling. Serve immediately.

EDNA BLINDELL • ST ALBANS, HERTFORDSHIRE

Broccoli Supreme

Serves 4-6

A quick and easy main course vegetarian dish. Serve it with crusty bread if you wish.

1 egg, beaten
300 g (10 oz) packet frozen chopped broccoli, partially thawed
225 g (8 oz) can cream-style corn
15 ml (1 tbsp) finely chopped or grated onion
salt and freshly ground black pepper
50 g (2 oz) butter
110 g (4 oz) packet herb seasoned stuffing mix

Preheat the oven to 180°C (350°F) mark 4. In a mixing bowl, combine the egg, broccoli, cream-style corn, onion, salt and pepper.

Melt the butter in a small saucepan, add the seasoned stuffing mix and toss to coat in the butter. Add three quarters of this to the vegetable mixture and stir until evenly mixed.

Turn the mixture into a 1.2 litre (2 pint) casserole. Sprinkle with the remaining buttered stuffing mix and bake uncovered in the preheated oven for 35-40 minutes. Serve immediately.

MAUREEN LIPMAN

LEFT: Mixed Rice Salad with Nuts and Apricots (page 81)
RIGHT: Spinach Dal (page 93)
BELOW: Hot Bean and Rice Salad with Pomegranates (page 84)

LEFT: Green Beans with Cumin (page 56)
RIGHT: Pumpkin Pancakes (page 33)
BELOW: Beetroot Julienne with Caraway (page 50)

ABOVE: Oyster Mushroom and Pine Nut Tartlets (page 96)
BELOW: Asparagus and Goat's Cheese Strudel (page 97)

ABOVE: Hazelnut Torte (page 150)
RIGHT: Raspberry and Honey Ice Cream (page 158)
BELOW: Glazed Saffron Cheesecakes (page 152)

That Veggy Quiche without Pastry

Serves 4-6

*I invented this recipe after I realised it was possible to make a quiche without pastry!
It goes well with a green salad and baked potatoes, garlic bread or granary bread. You
can vary the ingredients – try replacing the leeks and courgettes with vegetables of
your choice. To enrich the mixture, use half cream and half milk.*

about 45 ml (3 tbsp) vegetable oil
1 garlic clove, crushed
1 large onion, chopped
1-2 red peppers, cored, seeded and chopped
1 green pepper, cored, seeded and chopped
350 g (12 oz) leeks, sliced
125 g (4 oz) courgettes, sliced
125 g (4 oz) mushrooms, chopped
2 eggs
200 ml (⅓ pint) milk
good handful of chopped parsley
large pinch of freshly grated nutmeg
a little sea salt
plenty of freshly ground black pepper
125 g (4 oz) Cheddar cheese, grated
2 tomatoes, sliced

Preheat the oven to 180-190°C (350-375°F) mark 4-5. Heat the oil in a sauté
pan, add the garlic and onion and fry gently for a few minutes. Add the peppers,
leeks, courgettes and mushrooms and fry gently for about 5 minutes until
softened. Transfer the mixture to a lightly greased 25 cm (10 inch) flan dish.

In a bowl, whisk the eggs with the milk, then stir in the parsley, nutmeg,
seasoning and most of the cheese. Pour over the vegetables and arrange the
tomato slices on top. Sprinkle with the remaining cheese. Bake, uncovered, in
the preheated oven for 35-40 minutes until firm and lightly browned.

MRS J. O'BRIEN • BIRKENHEAD, MERSEYSIDE

Baked Feta Cheese and Spinach Omelette

Serves 4

This recipe was invented in desperation after a long day in the office! I like to serve it with a crisp green salad and daktyla (Greek bread) or baked potatoes.

250 g (9 oz) fresh spinach leaves, or frozen chopped spinach
4 eggs
200 ml (⅓ pint) skimmed milk
salt and freshly ground black pepper
200 g (7 oz) feta cheese

Preheat the oven to 190°C (375°F) mark 5. If using fresh spinach, rinse thoroughly, chop, then cook in a covered pan with just the water clinging to the leaves after washing until tender. Drain and leave to cool. If using frozen spinach, defrost, then squeeze out excess moisture.

In a bowl, whisk the eggs with the milk and seasoning. Crumble in the feta, then stir in the chopped spinach.

Transfer the mixture to a greased ovenproof dish and bake in the preheated oven for 30-40 minutes until golden brown and puffy. Serve immediately.

Shelagh Young • Witney, Oxfordshire

Cheesy Cauliflower Bake

Serves 2

The recipe was given to me by an American friend. I usually serve it as a main course, with a green salad and granary bread.

1 medium-large cauliflower, divided into florets
25 g (1 oz) butter
30 ml (2 tbsp) milk or single cream
2.5 ml (½ tsp) salt
freshly ground white pepper
50 g (2 oz) Emmenthal, Gruyère or Jarlsberg cheese, grated
1.25 ml (¼ tsp) freshly grated nutmeg
45 ml (3 tbsp) breadcrumbs
45 ml (3 tbsp) freshly grated Parmesan cheese

Preheat the oven to 180°C (350°F) mark 4. Steam or cook the cauliflower florets in boiling water until very tender. Drain thoroughly. Thoroughly mash the cauliflower and add the butter, milk or cream, salt, pepper and Emmenthal, Gruyère or Jarlsberg cheese, combining the ingredients well.

Transfer the mixture to a well buttered casserole. Mix together the nutmeg, breadcrumbs and Parmesan cheese, then sprinkle over the cauliflower mixture. Bake in the preheated oven for about 15 minutes until thoroughly heated through and bubbling. Serve immediately.

DAME JUDI DENCH

Mushroom Roulade

Serves 6-8

I prefer to serve this hot as a main course with a homemade tomato or parsley sauce, new potatoes and a salad or green vegetable, such as broccoli or spinach. If possible, use chestnut mushrooms for the roulade filling.

FOR THE ROULADE:
50 g (2 oz) fresh white breadcrumbs
175 g (6 oz) Gruyère cheese, finely grated
75 ml (5 tbsp) chopped mixed herbs
4 eggs, size 3, separated
150 ml (¼ pint) double cream
salt and freshly ground black pepper
30 ml (2 tbsp) warm water

FOR THE FILLING:
45 ml (3 tbsp) olive oil
2 garlic cloves, crushed
8 spring onions, finely sliced
350 g (12 oz) mushrooms, chopped
225 g (8 oz) feta cheese, crumbled
25 g (1 oz) cashew nuts, toasted and roughly chopped

To make the roulade, preheat the oven to 200°C (400°F) mark 6 and line a 23 x 33 cm (9 x 13 inch) Swiss roll tin with non-stick baking parchment. In a large bowl mix the breadcrumbs with all but 25 g (1 oz) of the cheese. Stir in the chopped herbs, egg yolks and cream. Season liberally with salt and pepper, then stir in the water. In a separate bowl, whisk the egg whites until stiff, but not dry. Using a large metal spoon, lightly fold them into the cheese mixture.

Pour the mixture into the lined Swiss roll tin, spreading it evenly into the corners. Bake in the preheated oven for 10-15 minutes until firm and well risen. Allow to cool in the tin while making the filling.

To make the filling, heat the oil in a frying pan. Add the garlic and spring onions and cook gently for 5 minutes until softened. Add the mushrooms and cook gently for 10 minutes. Remove from the heat and stir in the feta cheese, chopped nuts and seasoning to taste.

Sprinkle a sheet of greaseproof paper with the remaining 25 g (1 oz) grated cheese and turn the cooled roulade out on to the paper. Remove the lining paper. Carefully spoon the filling on to the roulade and spread evenly. Roll up from a short side as for a Swiss roll, using the greaseproof paper to help. Serve immediately, or allow to cool before serving.

LUCY DAY • HORSHAM, WEST SUSSEX

Root Vegetable Crumble

Serves 4

If any of the root vegetables are not available, simply make up the quantities with potatoes. If fresh horseradish is unavailable, you can use mustard, Tabasco, cayenne or chilli pepper to give the required spice. Any ground nuts can be used for the topping.

350 g (12 oz) parsnips
450 g (1 lb) carrots
225 g (8 oz) white turnips
225 g (8 oz) swede
2 medium onions
25 g (1 oz) vegetable margarine
600 ml (1 pint) vegetable stock
30 ml (2 tbsp) tomato purée
30 ml (2 tbsp) freshly grated horseradish

FOR THE TOPPING:
50 g (2 oz) vegetable margarine
50 g (2 oz) ground walnuts
50 g (2 oz) sesame seeds
50 g (2 oz) wheatgerm
60 ml (4 tbsp) chopped mixed herbs

Preheat the oven to 180°C (350°F) mark 4. Chop the parsnips, carrots, turnips and swede into 1 cm (½ inch) dice. Slice the onions thinly. Melt the margarine in a flameproof casserole and stir in all of the vegetables. Cover and allow to sweat for 10 minutes. Pour on the stock and bring to the boil. Stir in the tomato purée and horseradish. Cover the casserole and cook in the preheated oven for 30 minutes.

Meanwhile prepare the topping. Melt the margarine in a frying pan over a low heat. Stir in the rest of the ingredients and set aside. Remove the lid from the casserole and spoon the topping over the vegetables. Bake, uncovered, for 30 minutes.

CHRIS BONINGTON

Mexican Pepper Casserole

Serves 6

This delicious spicy casserole is served in the Moosewood Restaurant in Ithaca, New York. For a lighter version you can use half natural yogurt and half soured cream.

3 medium green peppers
3 medium red peppers
25 g (1 oz) butter
30 ml (2 tbsp) olive oil
2 medium onions, thinly sliced
3 garlic cloves, crushed
5 ml (1 tsp) salt
5 ml (1 tsp) ground cumin
5 ml (1 tsp) ground coriander
2.5 ml (½ tsp) mustard powder
1.25 ml (¼ tsp) chilli pepper, or to taste
30 ml (2 tbsp) flour
225 g (8 oz) Cheddar cheese, thinly sliced
4 large eggs
350 ml (12 fl oz) soured cream
paprika for sprinkling

Preheat the oven to 190°C (375°F) mark 5. Halve the peppers, remove the core and seeds, then slice the flesh into thin strips. Heat the butter and oil together in a sauté pan. Add the onions and garlic, then sprinkle with the salt, cumin, coriander, mustard powder and chilli pepper. Cook, stirring, until the onions are translucent, then add the peppers. Sauté over a low heat for about 10 minutes. Sprinkle in the flour and cook, stirring, until it is absorbed.

Spread half of the pepper mixture in a buttered deep casserole. Cover with half of the cheese slices. Add the rest of the pepper mixture, then top with the remaining cheese slices.

In a bowl, beat the eggs with the cream, then carefully pour over the cheese layer. Sprinkle with paprika. Cover and cook in the preheated oven for 40-45 minutes, removing the lid for the last 15 minutes to brown the top. Serve immediately.

MOLLIE KATZAN • NEW YORK

Vegetable and Lentil Casserole

Serves 4

This tasty casserole goes well with crunchy baked potatoes and – if you are cooking these – you might prefer to cook the casserole in the oven. It takes about an hour towards the bottom of an oven set at 200°C (400°F) mark 6.

700 g (1½ lb) mixed root vegetables, eg swede, carrot, turnip
45 ml (3 tbsp) oil
2 large onions, chopped
2 celery sticks, sliced
175 g (6 oz) orange lentils
2 garlic cloves, crushed
4 tomatoes, skinned
750 ml (1¼ pints) vegetable stock
salt and freshly ground black pepper
juice of ½ lemon
chopped parsley to garnish

Dice the root vegetables. Heat the oil in a large heavy-based pan or flameproof casserole. Add the root vegetables, onions and celery and cook gently for 5 minutes. Add the lentils and garlic and cook for a further 4-5 minutes, stirring frequently.

Add the tomatoes, stock and seasoning. Bring to the boil, then lower the heat, cover and cook gently for about 30 minutes until all of the vegetables are soft and the lentils are pale golden and soft. Add lemon juice to taste and check the seasoning. Serve hot, sprinkled with chopped parsley.

ROSE ELLIOT

Stuffed Cabbage Rolls

Serves 4

*These cabbage rolls baked in a cheese sauce make an ideal lunch, served
with a crisp green salad or buttered new potatoes. For this recipe, you really need
to use the larger cabbage leaves.*

½ medium white cabbage
1 medium onion, finely chopped
1 green or red pepper, cored, seeded and finely chopped
75 g (3 oz) mushrooms, finely chopped
1 courgette, finely chopped
125 g (4 oz) peanuts or cashew nuts, finely chopped
15 ml (1 tbsp) peanut butter
1 egg, beaten
5 ml (1 tsp) English mustard
2 Weetabix biscuits (approximately)
salt and freshly ground black pepper

FOR THE CHEESE SAUCE:
25 g (1 oz) butter
30 ml (2 tbsp) flour
400 ml (¾ pint) hot milk
75 g (3 oz) Cheddar cheese, grated

FOR THE TOPPING:
25 g (1 oz) Cheddar cheese, grated

Preheat the oven to 170°C (325°F) mark 3. Blanch the cabbage leaves in boiling
water for a few minutes. Drain and allow to cool.

To make the stuffing, mix together the onion, pepper, mushrooms, courgette
and nuts in a bowl. Stir in the peanut butter, beaten egg and mustard. Crumble
in enough Weetabix to give a moulding consistency. Season with salt and pepper.

Lay the cabbage leaves out on a work surface and divide the stuffing between
them. Roll up like pancakes, enclosing the filling. Place in an ovenproof dish.

To make the cheese sauce, melt the butter in a small pan and stir in the
flour. Cook, stirring, for 1-2 minutes, then remove from the heat and whisk in
the hot milk. Return to the heat and cook, stirring, until thickened. Off the
heat, add the cheese and stir until melted. Season with salt and pepper to taste.

Pour the cheese sauce over the cabbage rolls and sprinkle with the cheese
topping. Bake in the preheated oven for about 30 minutes. Serve hot.

EILEEN GILCHRIST • AMBLESIDE, CUMBRIA

Red Peppers with Chestnut Stuffing

Serves 8

This goes well with a leafy salad flavoured with walnuts and a Roquefort dressing. It can also be served with spanokopita (see page 106).

4 large red peppers
20 ml (4 tsp) olive oil
2 garlic cloves, finely chopped
24 black peppercorns

FOR THE FILLING:
½ x 425 g (15 oz) can unsweetened chestnut purée
1 egg
5 ml (1 tsp) cumin seeds
5 ml (1 tsp) celery seeds
5 ml (1 tsp) marigold bouillon
squeeze of lemon juice
salt and freshly ground black pepper
125 g (4 oz) oyster mushrooms, sliced
30 ml (2 tbsp) walnut oil
dash of soy sauce
30 ml (2 tbsp) sesame seeds

TO GARNISH:
coriander or parsley leaves

Preheat the oven to 190°C (375°F) mark 5. Halve the red peppers and remove the core and seeds. Place on a grill rack, skin side uppermost, and cook under a hot grill until the skins are slightly blackened.

Meanwhile to make the filling, mix the chestnut purée with the egg, cumin seeds and celery seeds. Flavour with marigold bouillon, lemon juice and seasoning to taste. Sauté the oyster mushrooms lightly in the walnut oil, then flavour with soy sauce to taste.

Turn the peppers over and put a little olive oil, garlic and 3 peppercorns in each one. Grill for 1-2 minutes. Divide the chestnut filling between the pepper halves. Cover with the mushroom mixture and sprinkle with sesame seeds. Bake in the preheated oven for 35-40 minutes. Serve garnished with coriander or parsley leaves.

ELISABETH ROUSSEL • WOODSTOCK, OXFORDSHIRE

Green Peppers
with Aubergine Stuffing

Serves 4

Serve these tasty baked peppers with a salad and plenty of crusty bread or rice.

1 large aubergine
90 ml (6 tbsp) oil
350 g (12 oz) passata
1 garlic clove, crushed
40 g (1½ oz) Parmesan cheese, freshly grated
salt and freshly ground black pepper
2 large green peppers

Preheat the oven to 180°C (350°F) mark 4. Peel the aubergine and cut into 1 cm (½ inch) cubes, discarding the ends. Heat the oil in a large frying pan, add the aubergine cubes and fry, stirring frequently, until softened.

Add the passata, garlic and half of the Parmesan cheese. Season with salt and pepper to taste. Stir well and simmer for 5 minutes.

Cut the green peppers in half and remove the core and seeds. Bring a large pan of water to the boil, add the pepper halves and blanch for 5 minutes. Drain thoroughly and place in a baking dish.

Fill the pepper halves with the aubergine mixture and sprinkle with the remaining Parmesan cheese. Bake in the preheated oven for 20 minutes.

Marrow with Crispy Stuffing

Serves 4

The crunchy nut stuffing contrasts well with the marrow in this protein-rich dish.

1 medium marrow
60 ml (4 tbsp) vegetable oil
175 g (6 oz) wholewheat breadcrumbs
175 g (6 oz) ground nuts, eg cashews nuts or walnuts
225 g (8 oz) button mushrooms, sliced
4 tomatoes, skinned and sliced
1 small onion, grated
salt and freshly ground black pepper

To GARNISH:
chopped parsley and tomato slices

Preheat the oven to 180°C (350°F) mark 4. Parboil the marrow in boiling water for 5 minutes, then drain. Cut in half lengthwise and scoop out the inside flesh and seeds to make a cavity in each half, leaving about a 2 cm (¾ inch) shell. Chop the marrow flesh, retaining the seeds if they are tender.

Heat the oil in a frying pan and add the breadcrumbs and ground nuts. Fry, stirring frequently, until crisp and golden, then add the mushrooms and fry gently until tender. Remove from the heat and add the chopped marrow, tomatoes, onion and seasoning.

Spoon the stuffing into each marrow half, pressing it firmly as you do so and piling it up well. Bake in the preheated for 30 minutes or until the marrow is tender and the filling is crisp. Serve immediately, garnished with chopped parsley and tomato slices.

ROSE ELLIOT

Potatoes with Creamy Tomato Sauce

Serves 6-8

This Columbian potato dish with its rich tomato and mozzarella sauce is substantial enough for a main dish. As a variation try serving the sauce over green beans, broccoli or cauliflower instead of potatoes.

8 large potatoes
30 ml (2 tbsp) margarine
6 spring onions
1 small onion, diced
5 tomatoes, skinned and coarsely chopped
125 ml (4 fl oz) cream
5 ml (1 tsp) finely chopped coriander leaves
1.25 ml (¼ tsp) dried oregano
pinch of ground cumin
2.5 ml (½ tsp) salt
freshly ground black pepper
125 g (4 oz) mozzarella cheese, grated

Cook the potatoes in their skins in boiling salted water until tender. Meanwhile melt the margarine in a frying pan and cut the spring onions into 2.5 cm (1 inch) lengths. Add the spring onions to the frying pan with the diced onion and tomatoes. Cook, stirring frequently, for about 5 minutes until soft and transparent.

Lower the heat and add the cream, coriander, oregano, cumin, salt and pepper to taste. Cook over a low heat, stirring constantly, until heated through. Add the cheese and continue stirring over a low heat until the cheese is melted.

Drain the cooked potatoes and place in a serving dish. Pour over the tomato sauce and serve immediately.

Broad Bean Cutlets with Onion Sauce

Serves 2 or 4

This recipe is used in Ryton Gardens Cafe at the National Centre for Organic Gardening. All proceeds from the cafe go to the HDRA charity which promotes organic, sustainable gardening and food production.

1 kg (2 lb) broad beans in the pod – 500 g (1 lb) shelled weight
sea salt and freshly ground black pepper
45 ml (3 tbsp) sunflower oil
1 small onion, finely chopped
1 hard-boiled egg, finely chopped
1 egg, beaten
75 g (3 oz) wholemeal breadcrumbs
5 ml (1 tsp) chopped basil
1 egg, beaten
wholemeal breadcrumbs for coating
150 ml (¼ pint) sunflower oil for frying

FOR THE ONION SAUCE:
25 g (1 oz) unsalted butter
1 large onion, chopped
25 g (1 oz) wholemeal flour
300 ml (½ pint) milk

Cook the broad beans in boiling salted water for 20 minutes. Drain well and work in a food processor to a coarse paste, or mash with a potato masher.

Heat the oil in a saucepan, and sauté the onion for 5 minutes. Remove from the heat. Add the bean paste and chopped hard-boiled egg; mix well. Stir in the beaten egg and breadcrumbs. Add the basil and seasoning to taste. Leave until cool enough to handle.

To make the onion sauce, melt the unsalted butter in a saucepan, add the onion and cook gently for 10-15 minutes. Remove from the heat and stir in the flour. Stir in the milk, a little at a time. Return to a low heat and stir constantly until the sauce is smooth and thickened. Add salt and pepper to taste.

Divide the broad bean mixture into 4 portions and shape into cutlets. Dip in egg, then coat with breadcrumbs. Heat the oil in a frying pan and shallow fry the cutlets for 2-5 minutes each side until crisp and golden brown. Drain on kitchen paper. Serve immediately with the onion sauce and vegetables.

JACKIE GEAR • RYTON ORGANIC GARDENS, COVENTRY

Mushroom Stroganoff

Serves 6

This may seem a large quantity of mushrooms, but they do reduce down considerably during cooking. It is important to cook them until the liquid has almost bubbled away. Serve the stroganoff with rice and seasonal green vegetables or a salad.

1.4 kg (3 lb) button mushrooms
50 g (2 oz) butter
30 ml (2 tbsp) light olive oil
1 onion, finely chopped
1 garlic clove, crushed
100 ml (3½ fl oz) dry white wine (optional)
15 ml (1 tbsp) cornflour
300 ml (½ pint) single cream
squeeze of lemon juice
sea salt and freshly ground black pepper

Wash the mushrooms, pat dry on absorbent kitchen paper, then slice thickly. Heat the butter and oil together in a large heavy-based pan. Add the onion and garlic, cover and cook gently for about 10 minutes until softened.

Add the mushrooms, stir well and cook for 20-30 minutes until all excess liquid has evaporated. Pour in the wine if using and let it bubble down until only a few spoonfuls of liquid remain.

Blend the cornflour with a little of the cream until smooth, then stir into the mushrooms with the rest of the cream. Slowly bring to the boil, stirring, and simmer for 2-3 minutes until thickened. Remove from the heat and stir in lemon juice and salt and pepper to taste. Serve immediately, with rice.

ROSE ELLIOT

Nut
Dishes

Pine Nut and Carrot Roast with Mushroom Sauce

Serves 4

25 g (1 oz) butter
1 onion, finely chopped
225 g (8 oz) carrots, finely grated
2 celery sticks, finely diced
225 g (8 oz) pine nuts, grated
30 ml (2 tbsp) chopped parsley
squeeze of lemon juice
2 eggs
sea salt and freshly ground black pepper
freshly grated nutmeg

FOR THE SAUCE:
7 g (¼ oz) dried mushrooms, rinsed
600 ml (1 pint) water
25 g (1 oz) butter
1 small onion, thinly sliced
10 ml (2 tsp) cornflour
30 ml (2 tbsp) Madeira
30 ml (2 tbsp) shoyu soy sauce

Preheat the oven to 180°C (350°F) mark 4. Grease a 500 g (1 lb) loaf tin and line the base and narrow sides with a strip of greased non-stick baking parchment. Melt the butter in a large pan and fry the onion, without browning, for 5 minutes, then add the carrot and celery, and cook, covered, for 10 minutes. Remove from heat and add the nuts, parsley, lemon juice and eggs. Season with plenty of salt, pepper and nutmeg to taste. Pour the mixture into the tin and bake for about 40 minutes, or until golden brown and firm in the centre.

To prepare the sauce, put the mushrooms in a saucepan with the water, bring to the boil, then remove from the heat and leave to soak for 30-50 minutes. Drain, reserving the liquid; chop the mushrooms. Melt the butter in a saucepan, add the onion and fry for 10 minutes, until lightly browned. Add the mushrooms and simmer for 30 minutes, until tender. Mix the cornflour with the reserved liquid, Madeira and shoyu, then add to the mushroom mixture. Bring to the boil, stirring, to thicken slightly. Season with salt and pepper.

To serve, turn the nut roast out on to a plate. Serve cut into thick slices with the mushroom sauce and lightly cooked vegetables.

ROSE ELLIOT

Mixed Nut Roast

Serves 4

As a vegetarian I usually enjoy a nut roast at Christmas.

25 g (1 oz) margarine
1 medium onion, chopped
125 g (4 oz) breadcrumbs
125 g (4 oz) hazelnuts
50 g (2 oz) walnuts
2 carrots, roughly chopped
2 celery sticks, roughly chopped
15 ml (1 tbsp) tomato ketchup
5 ml (1 tsp) Worcestershire sauce
few drops of Tabasco sauce
5 ml (1 tsp) curry powder
5 ml (1 tsp) dried mixed herbs
1 egg
salt and freshly ground black pepper
a little water to mix

Preheat the oven to 190°C (375°F) mark 5. Melt the margarine in a pan, add the onion and sweat gently until tender. Transfer the onion to a food processor and add the breadcrumbs, nuts, remaining vegetables, tomato ketchup, Worcestershire and Tabasco sauces, curry powder, herbs, egg and seasoning. Work the mixture to a dropping consistency, adding a little water to mix as necessary.

Transfer the mixture to a well greased 450 g (1 lb) loaf tin and bake in the oven for 1 hour. Turn out and cut into slices to serve.

RIGHT HON. BERNARD WEATHERILL • FORMER SPEAKER OF
THE HOUSE OF COMMONS

Pancakes with Tomato and Walnut Stuffing

Serves 4

Serve these tasty pancakes with a crisp leafy salad and wholewheat bread. For convenience you can make the pancakes in advance and keep covered in the refrigerator until required; they also freeze well.

FOR THE PANCAKES:
100 g (4 oz) plain flour
pinch of salt
2 eggs
200 ml (⅓ pint) creamy milk and water mixed
30 ml (2 tbsp) oil

FOR THE FILLING:
175 g (6 oz) walnuts
100 g (4 oz) fresh breadcrumbs
15 g (½ oz) butter
1 onion, chopped
1 garlic clove, crushed
5 ml (1 tsp) dried mixed herbs
6 medium tomatoes, skinned and chopped
sea salt and freshly ground black pepper

FOR THE CHEESE SAUCE:
25 g (1 oz) butter
30 ml (2 tbsp) flour
450 ml (¾ pint) hot milk
100 g (4 oz) Cheddar cheese, grated
freshly grated nutmeg

To make the pancake batter, put all the ingredients in a blender or food processor and whizz to a smooth cream. Alternatively sift the flour and salt into a bowl, add the eggs, then gradually beat in the milk, water and oil. Chill the batter in the refrigerator for 1 hour if possible.

To cook the pancakes, oil the base of a small frying pan, 15-18 cm (6-7 inches) in diameter, and place over a moderately high heat. When it is really hot, add about 30 ml (2 tbsp) oil and tilt the pan to coat the base evenly. Cook until the underside is crisp and golden brown, then turn and cook the other side. Turn out on to a sheet of greaseproof paper and allow to cool. Repeat

with remaining batter. Preheat the oven to 180°C (350°F) mark 4.

To make the filling, chop half of the walnuts and grind the rest in a blender or food processor. Mix the ground and chopped nuts in a bowl with the breadcrumbs. Melt the butter in a small pan, add the onion and fry gently until softened. Add the onion to the walnut mixture with the garlic, herbs and tomatoes. Mix well and season liberally with salt and pepper.

To make the cheese sauce, melt the butter in a saucepan, stir in the flour and cook, stirring, for 1-2 minutes. Remove from the heat and whisk in the hot milk. Return to the heat and whisk until thickened and smooth. Remove from the heat and stir in the cheese and nutmeg, salt and pepper to taste.

Divide the filling between the pancakes and roll up. Place them close together in a buttered shallow ovenproof dish into which they fit snugly. Pour the cheese sauce evenly over the pancakes and bake in the preheated oven for 20-30 minutes until piping hot.

ROSE ELLIOT

Aunt Bella's Nutmeat

Serves 6

This recipe has been in our family for at least 60 years. It was given to me when I married into a vegetarian family and became a vegetarian myself by my mother-in-law – known to her relatives as Aunt Bella. It is excellent served uncooked as a pâté or sandwich filling. It may also be lightly grilled, baked or fried, or used to stuff vegetables.

350 g (12 oz) mixed nuts, eg walnuts, cashews, brazils and hazelnuts
125 g (4 oz) dried wholemeal breadcrumbs
10 ml (2 tsp) Marmite
15 ml (1 tbsp) corn oil or vegetable margarine
300 ml (½ pint) mixed tomato juice and vegetable stock
1 small onion, grated
finely grated rind of 1 lemon
1 medium egg to bind (optional)

Grind the nuts with the breadcrumbs in a food processor, electric grinder or mincer. Put the Marmite and oil or margarine into a bowl. Heat the tomato juice and stock, then pour into the bowl, stirring to dissolve the Marmite and fat. Add the ground nuts and breadcrumbs, with the onion, lemon rind and egg if using. Mix thoroughly.

MRS JANIE WHITAKER • APPLETHWAITE, CUMBRIA

Nut Pâté

Serves 4

This is a personal adaptation of similar nut recipes found in many vegetarian cookbooks. It is suitable for vegans as long as you don't use butter to grease the pâté dish, and appeals to my non-vegetarian friends too.
I usually serve it as a starter with water biscuits, but you could also serve it as a light meal with crusty bread or toast and a green salad.

125 g (4 oz) blanched almonds
125 g (4 oz) brown breadcrumbs
2 spring onions or 1 small onion, finely chopped
1 garlic clove, crushed (optional)
30 ml (2 tbsp) chopped mixed herbs, eg parsley, chives, marjoram
salt and freshly ground black pepper
7.5 ml (1½ tsp) olive oil
tomato juice to mix
1 bay leaf

Grind the nuts with the breadcrumbs in a food processor, electric grinder or mincer. Add the chopped onion(s), garlic if using, herbs and seasoning to taste. Add the oil, then stir in enough tomato juice to give a stiff paste. (The amount of tomato juice required will depend on the freshness of the breadcrumbs.)

Turn the mixture into a lightly greased pâté dish and press the mixture down firmly. Put the bay leaf on top, cover and weight down. Chill in the refrigerator for 2 hours before serving.

BRIDGET WALKER • OXFORD

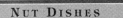
Vegi-burgers

Serves 6

This recipe has been passed down through several generations of my family. You can either bake the vegi-burgers as below, or fry them in a little oil turning halfway through cooking. I like to serve them with homemade tomato sauce, rice and a salad.

45 ml (3 tbsp) oil
3 onions, finely chopped
1 green pepper, cored, seeded and chopped
4-6 mushrooms, chopped
225 g (8 oz) packet tofu
15 ml (1 tbsp) chopped fresh mixed herbs, or 5 ml (1 tsp) dried
10 ml (2 tsp) tomato purée
salt and freshly ground black pepper
225-350 g (8-12 oz) mixed ground nuts and seeds, eg hazelnuts, cashew nuts,
pumpkin seeds and sesame seeds
175 g (6 oz) wholemeal breadcrumbs
1 egg, beaten
about 45 ml (3 tbsp) hot vegetable stock

Preheat the oven to 190°C (375°F) mark 5. Heat the oil in a frying pan. Add the onions and fry gently for about 5 minutes, then add the green pepper and mushrooms and fry gently until softened. Crumble in the tofu and fry gently, stirring, for 2-3 minutes. Add the herbs, tomato purée and seasoning.

Transfer the tofu mixture to a bowl and add the ground nuts and seeds, with the breadcrumbs. Mix in the beaten egg and sufficient hot stock to bind the mixture. Divide into 12 equal portions and shape into burgers. Place on a baking tray and cook in the preheated oven for about 20 minutes.

MARTHA YATES • MARLBOROUGH, WILTSHIRE

Peanut and Potato Rissoles

Serves 1-2

*These rissoles are an ideal way to use up leftover cooked potatoes. Serve them as a
tasty snack or a light meal with a salad.*

125 g (4 oz) potatoes
salt
cayenne pepper
10 ml (2 tsp) butter or margarine
10 ml (2 tsp) flour
22 ml (1½ tbsp) milk
30 ml (2 tbsp) finely ground peanuts
1 egg white, lightly beaten
seasoned breadcrumbs for coating
oil for deep-frying

Cut the potatoes into even-sized pieces and cook in boiling water until tender,
then drain. Mash until smooth, seasoning with salt and cayenne pepper to taste.

Melt the butter or margarine in a frying pan and stir in the flour. Gradually
stir in the milk and cook, stirring, until the mixture is thick. Remove from the
heat and add the potatoes and peanuts. Mix thoroughly.

Turn the mixture out onto a plate and divide into small balls. Dip in the egg
white, then roll in the seasoned breadcrumbs to coat thoroughly.

Heat the oil in a deep-fat fryer. When it is really hot, add the rissoles and
deep-fry until crisp and golden brown. Drain on absorbent kitchen paper.
Serve immediately.

Banana and Cashew Nut Curry

Serves 4

This unusual curry is flavoured with fresh and dried fruits, nuts and coconut cream. It is best served with plain boiled rice.

50 g (2 oz) butter or margarine
2 onions, chopped
1 apple, cored and chopped
50 g (2 oz) sultanas
50 g (2 oz) cashew nuts, finely chopped
25 g (1 oz) plain flour
25 g (1 oz) curry powder
175 ml (6 fl oz) water
175 ml (6 fl oz) milk
25 g (1 oz) creamed coconut
4 bananas, chopped
salt and freshly ground black pepper

Melt the butter or margarine in a large heavy-based pan. Add the onions and fry gently until softened and golden, then add the apple, sultanas and nuts.

Mix the flour and curry powder with a little of the water to a smooth paste. Add to the pan and cook, stirring continuously, for 3 minutes. Pour in the remaining water and milk. Stir in the coconut cream. Cook gently, stirring, until the mixture thickens.

Add the chopped bananas and season with salt and pepper to taste. Cook gently for 5 minutes. Serve immediately, with rice.

FLOELLA BENJAMIN

Pea and Cashew Nut Stew

Serves 4-6

Serve this tasty Indian dish with rice. As an alternative to reconstituting creamed coconut, you could use 125 ml (4 fl oz) frozen coconut cream, thawed.

450 g (1 lb) shelled fresh peas
salt and freshly ground black pepper
30 ml (2 tbsp) oil
225 g (8 oz) cashew nuts
8 small onions, chopped
2 garlic cloves, chopped
2.5 cm (1 inch) piece fresh root ginger, grated
1.25 ml (¼ tsp) garam masala
5 ml (1 tsp) rice flour
50 g (2 oz) block creamed coconut
¼ green pepper, seeded and chopped

Parboil the peas in lightly salted water for 2 minutes; drain, reserving the liquid.

Heat the oil in a frying pan, add the cashew nuts and fry, stirring constantly, until lightly browned. Remove with a slotted spoon and set aside. Add the onions to the pan and fry gently until softened, then add the garlic and ginger and cook for 1 minute. Stir in the garam masala, then the flour and cook for 1 minute.

Put the solid creamed coconut in a bowl and pour on about 200 ml (⅓ pint) of the reserved hot cooking water from the peas. Stir until the coconut is melted.

Add the coconut liquid to the pan with the peas, cashew nuts and green pepper. Stir to mix, then cook gently until the peas are cooked, adding a little more of the reserved cooking water to moisten if necessary. Serve immediately, with rice.

Cheesy Nut Rissoles

Makes 20

These deep-fried pastries make a delicious crunchy canapé – they are great with beer! Alternatively you could serve them as a light meal with a homemade tomato sauce, and a mixed salad.

175 g (6 oz) brazil nuts
175 g (6 oz) cashew nuts
75 g (3 oz) wholewheat flour
2.5 ml (½ tsp) salt
1 small onion, grated
125 g (4 oz) Cheddar cheese, grated
water to mix
125 g (4 oz) breadcrumbs
oil for deep-frying

Grind the brazil nuts and cashew nuts in a blender, food processor or electric grinder. Transfer to a bowl and stir in the flour, salt, onion and grated cheese. Add sufficient water to mix to a stiff dough.

Divide the mixture into 20 equal pieces and shape into patties. Roll in the breadcrumbs to coat thoroughly. Heat the oil in a deep-fat fryer. When it is really hot, deep-fry the rissoles in batches until crisp and golden brown. Drain on absorbent kitchen paper. Serve hot.

Nut Bobotie
with Cape Rice

Serves 4-6

The Cape Malay people of South Africa make a popular curried dish that combines fiery spices with different fruits to produce a rich meal with a distinctive flavour. The secret of a good bobotie lies in keeping the mixture very moist – and that is all the more important in this variation which uses a range of nuts. Serve this bobotie with Cape rice, a green salad, chutney, bananas with cinnamon, and grated coconut.

FOR THE BOBOTIE:
2 slices of white bread, crusts removed, cubed
300 ml (½ pint) milk
400 g (14 oz) mixed nuts, including peanuts, brazil nuts, walnuts and cashews
60 g (2½ oz) dried apricots, chopped
60 g (2½ oz) raisins
1 apple, cored and chopped
grated rind and juice of 1 lemon
10 ml (2 tsp) mustard powder
125 ml (4 fl oz) light red wine or fruit juice
25 g (1 oz) margarine
2 medium onions, chopped
2 garlic cloves, chopped
10 ml (2 tsp) ground coriander
10 ml (2 tsp) chilli powder, or to taste
75 g (3 oz) flaked almonds
1 egg
5 ml (1 tsp) turmeric

FOR THE CAPE RICE:
250 g (9 oz) long-grain rice
500 ml (16 fl oz) water
5 ml (1 tsp) salt
5 ml (1 tsp) turmeric
10 ml (2 tsp) sugar
50 g (2 oz) sultanas

Preheat the oven to 180°C (350°F) mark 4. Soak the bread in the milk. Grind the mixed nuts together.

In a large mixing bowl, combine the apricots, raisins and apple with the lemon rind and juice, mustard and wine or fruit juice.

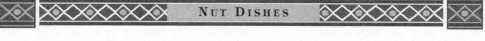

Melt the margarine in a deep pan, add the onions and garlic and sauté for 2 minutes. Mix the coriander and chilli powder together, add to the pan and cook over low heat, stirring, for 1 minute. Add the almonds and cook for a further 2 minutes, stirring constantly to avoid sticking.

Remove the bread from the milk and add it to the fruit mixture. Beat the egg with the turmeric and stir into the milk. Add the onion mixture to the fruit with a little of the yellow milk and mix thoroughly in the bowl to produce a consistent mixture.

Transfer the mixture to a greased shallow ovenproof dish. Pat flat, then pour over the rest of the milk. Cover and cook in the preheated oven for 1 hour.

To prepare the Cape rice, put all the ingredients into a saucepan, cover and bring to the boil. Simmer for about 20 minutes until all the water is absorbed and the rice is tender.

Serve the bobotie with the Cape rice and accompaniments.

RICHARD WALLACE • COTTERIDGE, BIRMINGHAM

Nutty Artichokes

Serves 2 or 4

I adapted this recipe from one given to me by a vegetarian friend. It serves 4 as a starter, or 2 as a main course accompanied by a crisp green vegetable.

450 g (1 lb) Jerusalem artichokes
225 g (8 oz) shallots, peeled
30 ml (2 tbsp) sunflower oil
125 g (4 oz) chopped walnuts
30 ml (2 tbsp) chopped parsley
5 ml (1 tsp) brown sugar
freshly ground black pepper

Peel the artichokes, rinse and if large cut into 2.5 cm (1 inch) pieces. Cook the artichokes and shallots separately in boiling water until cooked but still crisp. Drain well.

Heat the oil in a sauté pan, add the artichokes and shallots and cook over a medium heat for 3-4 minutes. Add the nuts, parsley, sugar and pepper to taste. Heat through and serve.

JUDITH HANN

Manomin Pancakes

Makes 36

*These make a wonderful breakfast. They are delicious with strawberries, blueberry
syrup or apple slices sautéed with cinnamon.*

FOR THE BATTER:
50 g (2 oz) wild rice, rinsed
5 ml (1 tsp) salt
25 g (1 oz) butter, melted
4 eggs, separated
300 ml (½ pint) milk
125 g (4 oz) blanched toasted almonds, finely chopped
125 g (4 oz) plain flour
pinch of cream of tartar

FOR FRYING:
about 25 g (1 oz) butter
about 30 ml (2 tbsp) oil

Bring 250 ml (8 fl oz) water to the boil in a medium saucepan. Add the wild
rice, cover and simmer over a low heat for about 45-55 minutes, until the rice is
tender and all the water is absorbed. Add the salt and melted butter.

Whisk the egg yolks until light in colour, then mix into the rice. Stir in the
milk, chopped nuts and flour. In a separate bowl, beat the egg whites with a
pinch of cream of tartar until stiff, but not dry. Fold into the batter. Preheat the
oven to 150°C (300°F) mark 2.

To cook the pancakes, melt 15 g (½ oz) butter with 15 ml (1 tbsp) oil in a
heavy-based frying pan or griddle over a medium heat. When it is hot, add
spoonfuls of the batter to the pan to form 6 cm (2½ inch) pancakes. Cook for
about 2-3 minutes until the edges are golden brown and the pancakes have
begun to set. Flip the pancakes to brown the other side, then remove. Repeat
with the remaining batter, adding more butter and oil to the griddle as
necessary. Arrange the hot pancakes in a single layer in an ovenproof dish; keep
warm in the oven until all the pancakes are cooked.

Serve the pancakes warm, with fruit, syrup or butter.

Puddings

Red Fruit Compote with Chocolate Terrine

Serves 6

This is an easy yet rather decadent pudding. Both the compote and terrine can be prepared a day ahead. You can use any red fruit for the compote, but cherries and strawberries are especially good. Use a quality chocolate for the terrine, such as Menier or Terry's.

FOR THE FRUIT COMPOTE:
1 kg (2 lb) red fruit, eg stoned black cherries or hulled strawberries
caster sugar for sprinkling
kirsch or cointreau to taste

FOR THE CHOCOLATE TERRINE:
250 g (9 oz) plain chocolate
300 ml (10 fl oz) double cream

To make the compote, slice the fruit, as necessary, then put into a shallow dish or bowl. Sprinkle with a little caster sugar to taste, and some liqueur – kirsch with cherries, cointreau with strawberries. Mix gently, then cover and leave for several hours, stirring from time to time.

Meanwhile, make the chocolate terrine. Line a 500 g (1 lb) loaf tin with a long strip of oiled non-stick baking parchment to cover the base and narrow sides. Break up the chocolate and put into a saucepan with the cream. Heat very gently until the chocolate has melted, then remove from the heat and leave to cool. When the mixture is really cool, whisk it hard until it thickens and changes colour slightly. Turn the mixture into the loaf tin. Cover and leave in the refrigerator for several hours, or overnight.

To serve, slip a knife round the sides of the terrine and turn it out, then cut into slices. Arrange one or two slices on each serving plate, with some of the red fruit compote alongside. Serve with extra whipped cream, if you want to be really indulgent!

ROSE ELLIOT

Peaches
in Spiced Wine

Serves 6

This is a delicious way to serve ripe flavourful peaches. You could also include a few plump raspberries, strawberries or redcurrants – adding them to the spiced wine with the peaches. Serve with single cream or Greek-style natural yogurt.

450 ml (¾ pint) red wine
50 ml (2 fl oz) water
2 cinnamon sticks
3 cloves
45 ml (3 tbsp) caster sugar
finely pared rind and juice of 1 orange
6 ripe peaches

Pour the red wine and water into a saucepan and add the spices, sugar, orange rind and juice. Heat gently for 4-6 minutes, then transfer to a non-metallic bowl.

Halve, stone and quarter the peaches. Place them skin side uppermost in the spiced wine and baste with the liquid. Cover and leave to macerate in a cool place but not the refrigerator for 3-4 hours or overnight, stirring occasionally.

Divide the fruit and wine between individual serving dishes, discarding the cinnamon, cloves and orange rind. Serve with cream or yogurt.

MOYRA FRASER • GOOD HOUSEKEEPING

Apple Almond

Serves 4

Having enjoyed this recipe for many years, I have made it countless times!
I use a square baking dish, measuring 18 x 20 x 7.5 cm (7 x 8 x 3 inches).

450 g (1 lb) cooking apples
about 30 ml (2 tbsp) water
75 g (3 oz) butter
100 g (4 oz) sugar
50 g (2 oz) ground almonds
1 egg, beaten

FOR THE TOPPING:
blanched almonds

Preheat the oven to 190°C (375°F) mark 5. Peel, core and slice the apples. Microwave or cook them in a covered pan over a low heat in the minimum of water until softened. Transfer the apples to a baking dish.

Melt the butter in a saucepan, then remove from the heat and stir in the sugar and ground almonds. Add the beaten egg and mix well. Spread the mixture over the apples and top with blanched almonds.

Bake in the preheated oven for about 30 minutes until the top is golden brown. Serve hot or cold, with cream.

MRS IVY MASTERS • RUSTINGTON, WEST SUSSEX

Fruit Crumble

Serves 4-6

This is a very quick and easy pudding. I make the crumble mixture in large quantities in my mixer, then store it in the freezer. The required amount can then be poured over the fruit and cooked from frozen.
You can use any combination of fruit. As variations, try rhubarb and ginger; blackberry and apple; or apples with raisins and cinnamon. The cooking time will depend on the fruit.

450 g (1 lb) mixed fresh fruit, eg apples, blackberries, blackcurrants, white currants and redcurrants
sugar to taste

FOR THE TOPPING:
125 g (4 oz) self-raising flour (preferably wholewheat)
50 g (2 oz) wheatgerm
75 g (3 oz) soft margarine
75 g (3 oz) demerara sugar

Preheat the oven to 180°C (350°F) mark 4. Prepare the fruit as necessary; hull the soft fruits; peel, core and slice the apples. Place in a pie dish and sweeten with sugar to taste.

To prepare the topping, mix the flour and wheatgerm together in a mixing bowl. Rub in the margarine until the mixture resembles breadcrumbs, then stir in the demerara sugar.

Spread the crumble topping evenly over the fruit in the pie dish. Bake in the preheated oven for 25-40 minutes until the fruit is tender and the crumble is crisp and lightly browned.

ANN MEERS • WELWYN GARDEN CITY, HERTFORDSHIRE

Peach and Almond Tranche

Serves 8

If the peaches aren't quite ripe, sprinkle a little sugar over them before topping with the almond-flavoured custard. For best results make the tranche no more than 8 hours before serving.

FOR THE PASTRY:
75 g (3 oz) butter, softened
75 g (3 oz) caster sugar
3 egg yolks
175 g (6 oz) plain white flour

FOR THE FILLING:
200 ml (⅓ pint) single cream
25 g (1 oz) ground almonds
350 g (12 oz) ripe peaches
15 g (½ oz) fresh white breadcrumbs
1 whole egg, plus 1 egg yolk
25 g (1 oz) caster sugar
50 g (2 oz) flaked almonds

TO FINISH:
icing sugar for dusting

First make the pastry. Cream together the butter, sugar and egg yolks. Gradually work in the flour and knead lightly until smooth. Wrap and chill in the refrigerator for about 30 minutes.

Roll out the pastry on a well floured surface and use to line a 34 x 11 cm (13½ x 4½ inch) loose-based fluted tranche tin. Chill for a further 30 minutes. Meanwhile preheat the oven to 190°C (375°F) mark 5.

Line the flan case with a piece of greaseproof paper and beans. Bake blind for 10-15 minutes. Remove the paper and beans and return to the oven for a further 5 minutes until the base is golden and well dried out. Lower the oven temperature to 180°C (350°F) mark 4.

Meanwhile make the filling. Put the cream and ground almonds in a saucepan and slowly bring almost to the boil. Take off the heat, cover and leave to infuse for about 30 minutes.

Quarter the peaches, discarding the stones. Carefully peel each quarter and

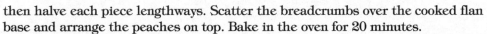
then halve each piece lengthways. Scatter the breadcrumbs over the cooked flan base and arrange the peaches on top. Bake in the oven for 20 minutes.

Whisk the whole egg and egg yolk with the sugar. Strain the infused cream into the mixture, stirring. Pour the custard mixture over the peaches and sprinkle with the flaked almonds.

Return to the oven and bake for a further 25-30 minutes, or until the custard is set and the nuts lightly browned.

Immediately dust the tranche liberally with icing sugar. If you like, heat three or four long metal skewers over a gas flame or electric ring until red hot. Holding them with oven gloves press a lattice pattern into the icing sugar and nuts. The sugar will burn and caramelise immediately, leaving an attractive pattern on the tranche. Serve warm or cold, with single cream.

MOYRA FRASER • GOOD HOUSEKEEPING

Pommes au Beurre

Serves 4

Use hard, sweet eating apples for this quick and easy dessert. You will need to prepare about 700 g (1½ lb) to give the weight below. To make vanilla sugar, simply store a vanilla pod in a jar of caster sugar to impart flavour.

450 g (1 lb) peeled, quartered and cored apples (prepared weight)
25 g (1 oz) butter
25 g (1 oz) caster sugar or vanilla sugar

Cut the apples evenly into thin slices. Melt the butter in a frying pan and add the apples with the sugar. Cook gently until the apples are pale golden and translucent. Turn the slices very gently during cooking, or shake the pan rather than stir if they are closely packed, to avoid breaking them up. Serve hot.

SIR KNOX CUNNINGHAM

Baked Orange Pears with Spiced Cream

Serves 6

This is a delicious way to serve pears – in a tangy orange sauce, accompanied by a sweetened ginger cream.

6 fresh firm pears

FOR THE SAUCE:
20 g (¾ oz) arrowroot
55 g (2¼ oz) sugar
tiny pinch of salt
375 ml (12 fl oz) orange juice

FOR THE SPICED CREAM:
250 ml (8 fl oz) double cream
55 g (2¼ oz) sugar
pinch of ground ginger
pinch of ground allspice

Preheat the oven to 180°C (350°F) mark 4. To make the sauce, mix the arrowroot with the sugar, salt and a little of the orange juice in a small pan. Add the remaining orange juice, stirring well. Slowly bring to the boil, stirring to dissolve the sugar, then lower the heat and cook, stirring, for about 1 minute until thickened and clear. Remove from the heat.

Carefully remove the cores from the bottom of the pears, leaving the stems intact. Peel the top two thirds of each one. Place the pears in a baking dish and pour the hot orange sauce over them. Bake in the preheated oven for 30-45 minutes until the pears are tender, basting with the sauce several times during cooking.

Meanwhile to prepare the spiced cream, lightly whip the cream with the sugar, ginger and allspice. Chill in the refrigerator until required.

Serve the pears hot or chilled, with the spiced cream.

AMERICAN EMBASSY

Yummy Yams

Serves 6-8

A good source of vitamin A, yams are especially nice combined with apples in this original pudding.

8 yams, peeled and diced
squeeze of lemon juice
125 g (4 oz) butter, melted
125 ml (4 fl oz) golden syrup
75 ml (5 tbsp) brown sugar
30 ml (2 tbsp) dry sherry
5 ml (1 tsp) ground cinnamon
salt
2 cooking apples

Cook the yams in boiling water with a little lemon juice added to prevent discolouration for 20 minutes or until tender. Drain well. Preheat the oven to 180°C (350°F) mark 4.

Put the cooked yams in a food processor or blender with 90 ml (6 tbsp) melted butter, the syrup, brown sugar, sherry, cinnamon and salt. Purée until smooth.

Peel, quarter and core the apples, then cut into slices. Spread half of the yam mixture in a buttered 1.75 litre (3 pint) pie dish or flan tin. Arrange half of the apple slices over the yams. Repeat the layers. Brush the top layer of the apples with the remaining 30 ml (2 tbsp) melted butter. Bake in the oven for about 30 minutes or until the apples are golden brown but still retaining their shape. Serve immediately.

Hazelnut Torte

Serves 8

This recipe was given to me by an Austrian lady living in the same village in Cheshire, around 1950.

75 g (3 oz) low-fat margarine
75 g (3 oz) soft brown sugar
1 egg
125 g (4 oz) ground hazelnuts
125-150 g (4-5 oz) plain flour (or use a mixture of plain and wholewheat flour)
45-60 ml (3-4 tbsp) apricot jam

To FINISH:
icing sugar for dusting

Preheat the oven to 180°C (350°F) mark 4. In a mixing bowl, cream the margarine with the sugar until light and fluffy. Beat in the egg. Stir in the hazelnuts, then mix in sufficient flour to give a fairly soft dough (not as firm as a pastry dough).

Cut off a small amount and set aside for the lattice. Shape the rest of the dough into a round and place in an oiled 18 cm (7 inch) sandwich tin. Spread with the apricot jam. Roll out the remaining dough and cut into strips. Arrange in a lattice pattern over the jam.

Bake in the preheated oven for about 20 minutes until the lattice topping is crisp and golden brown. Sprinkle with icing sugar while still hot. Allow to cool before serving.

DOREEN PLEYDELL • KNUTSFORD, CHESHIRE

Beverley Hills Cheesecake

Serves 8-10

A rich, tempting and creamy baked cheesecake, flavoured with vanilla, on a crunchy biscuit base.

FOR THE BISCUIT CRUST:
125 g (4 oz) plain crunchy biscuits
125 g (4 oz) ginger biscuits
125 g (4 oz) unsalted butter

FOR THE CHEESE LAYER:
3 x 200 g (7 oz) packets Philadelphia cream cheese
175 g (6 oz) caster sugar
2 eggs, beaten
2.5 ml (½ tsp) vanilla flavouring

FOR THE TOPPING:
150 ml (5 fl oz) soured cream
15 ml (1 tbsp) caster sugar
2.5 ml (½ tsp) vanilla flavouring

To make the biscuit crust, crush the plain and ginger biscuits together in a food processor or with a rolling pin. Set aside a large handful for the topping. Melt the butter, then mix with the rest of the biscuit crumbs. Press the crumb mixture into the base of a 23 cm (9 inch) loose-bottomed springform cake tin.

To prepare the cheese layer, in a bowl cream the cheese with the sugar until evenly blended. Gradually beat in the eggs and vanilla flavouring to give a smooth mixture.

Pour the cheese mixture over the biscuit crust and place in a cold oven. Set the oven to 180°C (350°F) mark 4 and when this temperature is reached, bake for 30 minutes. Turn off the oven and leave the cheesecake to cool in the oven for about 30 minutes. Remove from the oven and set the temperature to 260°C (500°F) mark 10.

To make the topping, mix the soured cream with the sugar and vanilla flavouring. Pour over the cheesecake and sprinkle with the reserved crumbs. Bake in the preheated oven for 5 minutes.

Allow to cool, then chill in the refrigerator overnight. Carefully remove the cheesecake from the tin and cut into wedges to serve.

JACK HAWKINS

Glazed Saffron Cheesecakes

Serves 6

I used deep muffin rings to mould the cases for these delicious cheesecakes, but you could use shallower 10 cm (4 inch) rings. The cheesecakes can be made ahead and kept covered in a cool place for up to 8 hours; decorate and glaze no more than 1 hour before serving.

FOR THE PASTRY:
175 g (6 oz) plain white flour
75 g (3 oz) butter or margarine
25 g (1 oz) caster sugar
about 30 ml (2 tbsp) chilled water

FOR THE FILLING:
60 ml (4 tbsp) double cream
pinch of saffron strands
75 g (3 oz) low-fat soft cheese
75 g (3 oz) natural cottage cheese
1 egg, separated
5 ml (1 tsp) cornflour
finely grated rind of ½ lemon
15 ml (1 tbsp) lemon juice
25 g (1 oz) caster sugar

FOR THE TOPPING:
3 small ripe nectarines
90 ml (6 tbsp) redcurrant jelly

To make the pastry, sift the flour into a bowl, rub in the fat until the mixture resembles breadcrumbs, then stir in the sugar. Add sufficient water to bind the pastry.

Roll out the pastry thinly and use to line six 8.5 cm (3¼ inch) deep muffin rings placed on a baking sheet. Chill for about 30 minutes. Preheat the oven to 200°C (400°F) mark 6.

Line the pastry cases with greaseproof paper and beans, then bake blind for about 10 minutes until well dried out. Remove the hoops and return to the oven until the pastry is well browned. Replace the muffin rings. Lower the oven temperature to 180°C (350°F) mark 4.

Meanwhile, warm the cream with the saffron, take off the heat, cover and leave to infuse for 15 minutes. Place the cheeses, egg yolk, cornflour, lemon rind and juice in a food processor or blender and process briefly until smooth and quite thick. In a bowl, whisk the egg white until stiff but not dry, then gradually whisk in the sugar, keeping the mixture stiff. Fold into the blended cheese mixture.

Divide the cheesecake mixture between the pastry cases. Bake in the oven for about 25 minutes or until lightly set. Allow to cool, then carefully remove the hoops.

Halve and stone the nectarines, then slice thinly. Arrange on the cheese-cakes. In a small saucepan gently heat the redcurrant jelly with 15 ml (1 tbsp) water until smooth. Bring to the boil and reduce slightly until syrupy. Brush the hot jelly evenly over the fruits to cover completely.

MOYRA FRASER • GOOD HOUSEKEEPING

Baked Bananas

Serves 4

These delicious baked bananas flavoured with lime or lemon juice are wonderful served with soured cream. If preferred you can sweeten them with honey instead of sugar.

4 medium semi-ripe bananas
about 40 g (1½ oz) butter
brown sugar to taste
lemon or lime juice to taste

Preheat the oven to 180°C (350°F) mark 4. Peel the bananas and place them in a buttered baking dish. Dot them with butter. Sprinkle liberally with brown sugar and lemon or lime juice.

Bake in the oven for 40 minutes, turning the bananas and basting them with the juices halfway through cooking. Serve immediately, with soured cream if you like.

Chocolate Mousse

Serves 6

This mousse is best made on the day you wish to serve it and kept in a cool place, but not the refrigerator, until required.

225 g (8 oz) plain chocolate
150 ml (¼ pint) double cream
5 eggs, size 3 (or 4 size 1 eggs), separated
25 g (1 oz) caster sugar
45 ml (3 tbsp) rum

To DECORATE:
about 90 ml (6 tbsp) double cream, whipped
grated or flaked chocolate

Break up the chocolate and put it into a heatproof bowl with the cream. Stand the bowl over a pan of hot but not boiling water, and stir until the chocolate is melted. Take off the heat.

In another bowl, beat the egg yolks with the caster sugar until pale and creamy, then gradually whisk in the melted chocolate. Stand this bowl over the pan of hot water and whisk for about 5 minutes until the mixture is thick and creamy. Take it off the heat and add the rum.

In a separate bowl, whisk the egg whites until stiff, then fold them into the mixture. Turn into a glass bowl and leave in a cool place for 1 hour.

Just before serving, decorate the mousse with whipped cream and grated or flaked chocolate.

MISS A. LOWRY

Chocolate Pots with Mint Cream

Serves 6

These delicious chocolate pots are ideal to serve as a dinner party dessert. They are quick to prepare but you need to allow plenty of time for them to chill and set.

200 g (7 oz) plain chocolate (preferably Menier)
25 g (1 oz) butter
5 eggs, separated
150 ml (¼ pint) whipping cream
few drops of peppermint essence

TO DECORATE:
chocolate mints

Break up the chocolate and put it into a large heatproof bowl with the butter. Stand the bowl over a pan of gently simmering water and leave until the chocolate has melted, stirring once or twice.

Meanwhile, in a separate bowl whisk the egg whites until stiff. Remove the bowl of chocolate from the pan and stir in the egg yolks. Stir in a spoonful of the egg white, then very lightly fold in the remainder using a large metal spoon.

Divide the mixture between 6 individual dishes, cover and chill in the refrigerator for 6 hours until firm.

Just before serving, whip the cream in a bowl until it forms soft peaks, then fold in the peppermint essence. Spoon or pipe on top of the chocolate pots. Decorate with chocolate mints.

ROSE ELLIOT

Pavlova

Serves 4

A crisp, light meringue is the perfect base upon which to serve flavourful fruits.
Choose whichever fruits are in season: try a mixture of strawberries, raspberries and
blueberries; or tropical fruits, such as pineapple, passionfruit and kiwi fruit.

2 egg whites
50 g (2 oz) caster sugar
5 ml (1 tsp) cornflour
5 ml (1 tsp) white vinegar
few drops of vanilla flavouring (optional)

FOR THE TOPPING:
100-125 ml (3½-4 fl oz) double cream
about 300 g (10 oz) prepared fresh fruit

Preheat the oven to 160°C (325°F) mark 3. Grease a dinner plate and cover with greaseproof paper, then place under cold running water until thoroughly wet. Leave to drain.

In a bowl, whisk the egg whites until stiff, then whisk in the sugar 15 ml (1 tbsp) at a time, keeping the mixture stiff. Beat in the cornflour, then add the vinegar and vanilla flavouring if using. Beat for 1 minute to yield a thick, glossy meringue.

Spoon the meringue on to the prepared plate and spread evenly to 2.5 cm (1 inch) from the edge of the plate. Bake in the preheated oven for 15 minutes until rising and almost beginning to brown, then lower the oven temperature to 150°C (300°F) mark 2 and bake for a further 30-45 minutes until crisp. While it is still hot, carefully remove the lining paper. Allow to cool.

Just before serving, whip the cream until thick and spread over the cold pavlova. Top with the fruits and serve immediately.

T. PATRICK BRAND

Rum Ice Cream

Serves 6

*Serve this rich, creamy ice cream scooped into glass dishes, with wafers
or crisp dessert biscuits if you wish.*

3 eggs
50 g (2 oz) caster sugar
600 ml (1 pint) milk
300 ml (½ pint) double cream
30 ml (2 tbsp) dark sweet Jamaica rum

Beat the eggs lightly in a large heatproof bowl, then add the sugar and whisk
until well blended. Warm the milk in a saucepan, then pour on to the egg
mixture, stirring constantly.

Place the bowl over a pan of simmering water and stir constantly until the
custard thickens. Do not allow the custard to boil or it will curdle. Remove the
bowl from the pan and allow to cool.

Whisk the cream and rum into the cold custard. Transfer the mixture to an
ice-cream maker and churn for 20-30 minutes until firm. If you do not have an
ice-cream maker, pour the mixture into a shallow freezer container and freeze,
whisking several times during freezing to break down the ice crystals.

Allow the ice cream to soften at cool room temperature for 15-20 minutes
before serving.

MRS O. McCONNELL

Raspberry and Honey Ice Cream

Serves 4

You can use a different soft fruit purée for this ice cream, but I think raspberries work best. To make the purée, simply whizz about 225 g (8 oz) raspberries in a blender or food processor, then pass through a sieve to remove the pips.

125 ml (4 fl oz) raspberry purée
250 ml (8 fl oz) double cream or thick yogurt
15 ml (1 tbsp) lemon juice
60 ml (4 tbsp) thin honey
pinch of salt
2 egg whites

In a bowl, mix the raspberry purée with the cream or yogurt. Add the lemon juice, honey and salt, mixing thoroughly. Turn the mixture into a shallow freezer tray and freeze until semi-frozen.

Remove from the freezer and turn into a bowl. Beat until smooth, breaking down the ice crystals. In a separate bowl, whisk the egg whites until stiff, then fold into the raspberry mixture.

Return to the freezer tray, cover and freeze until firm.

BARBARA CARTLAND

Breads, Biscuits & Cakes

Easy Homemade Bread

Makes one 900 g (2 lb) loaf

A wholewheat loaf, made by the quick, one-rise method, is no more difficult to make than a simple cake – in fact, I think it's easier – and the light, moist bread is a delight. I like using fresh yeast because it smells so pleasant and works so quickly, but you could use the easy-mix dried yeast, which you simply mix with the flour, if you prefer. You can buy fresh yeast from most bakers and some supermarket bakeries. If you want to make a bigger batch of bread, using a 1.5 kg (3¼ lb) bag of flour, use double the amount of yeast and three times all the other quantities.

500 g (1 lb 2 oz) wholewheat flour
5 ml (1 tsp) brown sugar
10 ml (2 tsp) sea salt
15 g (½ oz) fresh yeast
about 13 fl oz (380 ml) tepid water
kibbled wheat or extra flour for coating

First, grease one 900 g (2 lb) or two 450 g (1 lb) loaf tins generously with butter or white vegetable fat. Next put the flour, sugar and salt into a bowl and warm them in a cool oven for a few minutes – this will help the yeast to work faster.

Crumble the yeast into a small bowl, then pour in a little of the water and leave it for a minute or two until the yeast is soft, then blend it with the water. Make a well in the flour mixture and pour in the yeast and water mixture, and the remaining water. Mix well, first using a spoon and then your hands, until you have a soft dough which leaves the sides of the bowl clean.

Turn the dough out on to a board or working surface sprinkled with kibbled wheat and press it out into a rectangle the same width as the length of the tin (or divide the dough into two pieces if you are using two tins). Gently roll the rectangle up, like a Swiss Roll, and put it, seam-side down, into the tin. Press the dough down into the corners so that the middle comes up into a nice dome shape.

Put the bread into a warm place, cover with a polythene carrier bag or damp cloth, and leave it until the dome of the bread has risen level with the top of the tin or tins. The timing will depend on the temperature; it may be as little as 30 minutes if the bread is in a warm place, or an hour or more at room temperature – longer if it's really cool.

When it's ready, bake the bread in a preheated oven at 200°C (400°F) mark 6 for 45 minutes, or 35 minutes for small loaves. Then turn the bread out of the tin(s) and pop it back into the oven, upside down, for about 5 minutes, to make the sides crisp. Cool on a wire rack.

Rose Elliot

Healy's Cottage Bread

Makes one medium-large loaf

This nutritious, quick and easy to prepare cottage bread fulfils all my criteria for a good recipe. The ingredients are easy to obtain, and its simplicity and wholesome nature make it ideal for inclusion in this cookbook.

15 ml (1 tbsp) dried yeast
450 ml (¾ pint) warm water
15-30 ml (1-2 tbsp) olive oil
15-30 ml (1-2 tbsp) honey or molasses
700 g (1½ lb) strong plain wholewheat flour
10 ml (2 tsp) salt
10 ml (2 tsp) caraway seeds (optional)
10 ml (2 tsp) sunflower seeds

TO FINISH:
a little milk or salted water for brushing
sunflower seeds for sprinkling (optional)

Sprinkle the dried yeast into the warm water in a small bowl. Add the olive oil and honey or molasses and leave in a warm place for 10-15 minutes until frothy.

Place the flour in a large bowl with the salt, caraway if using, and sunflower seeds, make a well in the centre and pour in the yeast liquid. Using a wooden spoon, gradually work the flour into the yeast liquid until evenly mixed. Then, using the spoon, vigorously knock the dough back and forth 80-100 times to trap in sufficient air.

Cover the bowl with a damp cloth and leave to rise in a warm place for about 1 hour until doubled in size.

Knock back the dough with the wooden spoon, cover and leave for about 15 minutes. Preheat the oven to 180°C (350°F) mark 4.

Shape three quarters of the dough into a round and place on a greased baking sheet. Shape the remaining piece into a smaller round and place on top of the larger round. Press your forefinger down through the middle of the dough. Brush with a little milk or salted water and sprinkle with sunflower seeds if desired. Bake in the preheated oven for 45 minutes. Turn out and cool on a wire rack.

KAFFE FASSETT

Cheese and Celery Loaf

Makes one 450 g (1 lb) loaf

This is a delicious alternative to the ubiquitous garlic bread! It can be served with almost any vegetarian meal, and is particularly good with soups.

300 g (10 oz) self-raising flour
5 ml (1 tsp) salt (optional)
50 g (2 oz) margarine
2 celery sticks, finely chopped
125 g (4 oz) Cheshire cheese, grated
1 garlic clove, crushed
1 egg, size 1 or 2, beaten
200 ml (⅓ pint) milk

Preheat the oven to 190°C (375°F) mark 5. Grease a 450 g (1 lb) loaf tin. Sift the flour, and salt if using, into a mixing bowl. Rub in the margarine until the mixture resembles fine breadcrumbs. Add the celery, cheese and garlic and mix well. Stir in the beaten egg and milk.

Mix well and knead lightly to a soft dough. Turn into the greased loaf tin and cook in the preheated oven for 50 minutes to 1 hour until well risen and golden brown on top. Turn out and cool on a wire rack.

MS MARGY WELTON • HULL, NORTH HUMBERSIDE

Cheese Biscuits

Makes about 24

125 g (4 oz) plain flour
pinch of salt
pinch of cayenne pepper
50 g (2 oz) butter
25 g (1 oz) Cheddar cheese, grated
25 g (1 oz) Parmesan cheese, freshly grated
a little beaten egg yolk to mix
a little water to mix

Preheat the oven to 200°C (400°F) mark 6. Sift the flour, salt and cayenne pepper into a bowl. Rub in the butter until the mixture resembles fine breadcrumbs. Stir in the grated cheese. Mix the egg yolk with the water and add sufficient to bind the mixture to a stiff paste.

Knead lightly, then roll out thinly on a lightly floured surface. Prick well with a fork then cut into rounds or other shapes with a pastry cutter or sharp knife. Place the biscuits on lightly greased baking sheets and chill for 15 minutes.

Bake in the preheated oven for 7-10 minutes. Leave on the baking sheets for 1 minute, then transfer to a wire rack to cool.

Irish Shortbread

Makes 16 pieces

225 g (8 oz) plain flour
125 g (4 oz) cornflour
50 g (2 oz) caster sugar
225 g (8 oz) butter
caster sugar for sprinkling

Preheat the oven to 170°C (325°F) mark 3. Sift the flours into a bowl and stir in the sugar. Melt the butter in a saucepan, then add to the dry ingredients and mix well. Knead to a smooth dough.

Divide the dough in half and press each piece into an 18 cm (7 inch) sandwich tin. Bake in the preheated oven for 30 minutes. Increase the oven temperature to 190°C (370°F) mark 5.

Mark each shortbread into 8 sections and sprinkle with caster sugar. Return to the oven and bake for a further 15 minutes. Leave in the tin for 5 minutes, then carefully transfer to a wire rack to cool. Divide into wedges to serve.

MRS J.A. LYNN

Treacle and Date Scones

Makes 8

These scones are light, semi-sweet, and make a healthy snack for kids.

15 ml (1 tbsp) black treacle
60 ml (4 tbsp) milk or soy milk
10 ml (2 tsp) fine oatmeal
125 g (4 oz) plain wholewheat flour
pinch of salt
10 ml (2 tsp) baking powder
25 g (1 oz) brown sugar
25 g (1 oz) butter or margarine, in pieces
25 g (1 oz) cooking dates, chopped

Preheat the oven to 180°C (350°F) mark 4. Put the treacle and milk into a small saucepan and warm until they blend together, then remove from the heat and leave to cool.

Meanwhile, sift together the oatmeal, flour, salt and baking powder into a mixing bowl. Add the sugar, then rub in the fat until the mixture resembles breadcrumbs. Add the dates and the cooled treacle and milk, and mix to a soft pliable consistency.

Shape the scone mixture into a round on a floured baking sheet and mark into 8 sections. Bake in the preheated oven for 15 minutes. Cool on a wire rack. Serve warm or cold.

ROSE ELLIOT

Chocolate Macaroon Fingers

Makes about 24

125 g (4 oz) cooking chocolate
2 eggs
225 g (8 oz) caster sugar
125 g (4 oz) desiccated coconut
10 ml (2 tsp) plain flour
50 g (2 oz) glacé cherries, chopped

Preheat the oven to 150°C (300°F) mark 2. Grease a 33 x 23 cm (13 x 9 inch) Swiss roll tin and line with greaseproof paper. Break up the chocolate into a heatproof bowl and place over a pan of simmering water until melted. Spread evenly over the base of the tin and leave to cool.

In a mixing bowl, beat the eggs. Add the sugar, coconut and flour and beat well until evenly mixed. Stir in the cherries. Spread evenly over the chocolate in the tin.

Bake in the preheated oven for 15-20 minutes. Leave to cool in the tin. Cut into fingers or squares to serve.

MISS A.A.H. LAMONT

Lancashire Parkin

Makes 12-16 slices

I first tasted this Lancashire Parkin when I met my future in-laws for the first time in 1941. It's a good filling gingerbread and has always been a firm picnic favourite on our country walks.

300 g (10 oz) golden syrup, or half syrup, half black treacle
125 g (4 oz) butter
125 g (4 oz) sugar
225 g (8 oz) plain wholemeal flour
225 g (8 oz) rolled oats
5 ml (1 tsp) ground ginger
pinch of salt
2.5 ml (½ tsp) bicarbonate of soda
150 ml (¼ pint) milk

Preheat the oven to 180°C (350°F) mark 4. Grease a 23 x 18 cm (9 x 7 inch) tin and line the base with greaseproof paper. Put the syrup, butter and sugar in a small saucepan and heat gently until melted. Meanwhile, in a mixing bowl mix the flour, rolled oats, ginger and salt together. Make a well in the centre. Pour in the melted mixture and mix thoroughly.

Dissolve the bicarbonate of soda in the milk, then add to the mixture and stir well until evenly blended. Turn into the prepared tin.

Bake in the preheated oven for about 50 minutes to 1 hour, or until slightly shrunk away from the edges of the tin. Turn out and cool on a wire rack.

MRS EVELYN JOHNSTON • HADLEIGH, ESSEX

Nutty Slack

Makes about 32 squares

This is one of my favourite family recipes from Ireland.

225 g (8 oz) chopped dates
5 ml (1 tsp) bicarbonate of soda
60 ml (4 tbsp) hot water
225 g (8 oz) margarine or butter
30 ml (2 tbsp) golden syrup
175 g (6 oz) rolled oats
175 g (6 oz) sugar
175 g (6 oz) self-raising flour
175 g (6 oz) desiccated coconut

Preheat the oven to 180°C (350°F) mark 4. Line a 30 x 23 cm (12 x 9 inch) Swiss roll tin with non-stick baking parchment.

In a small bowl, mix the dates with the bicarbonate of soda and hot water. Put the margarine or butter and syrup in a small saucepan and heat gently until melted.

In a large mixing bowl stir together the rolled oats, sugar, flour and coconut. Make a well in the centre and pour in the melted ingredients. Add the date mixture. Mix all the ingredients together until evenly blended. Turn into the prepared tin and spread evenly.

Bake in the preheated oven for about 30 minutes until golden brown. Leave in the tin for 15 minutes then mark into squares while still warm. Cool completely in the tin.

MRS PAT FERGUSON • EDINBURGH

Date Squares

Makes 36 squares

First make the date filling, then while it is cooling prepare the rolled oats mixture.

FOR THE DATE FILLING:
250 ml (8 fl oz) water
75 g (3 oz) brown sugar
350 g (12 oz) chopped dates
1.25 ml (¼ tsp) lemon juice

FOR THE ROLLED OATS MIXTURE:
225 g (8 oz) butter
175 g (6 oz) brown sugar
350 g (12 oz) plain flour
1.25 ml (¼ tsp) salt
1.25 ml (¼ tsp) bicarbonate of soda
30 ml (2 tbsp) water
175 g (6 oz) rolled oats

Preheat the oven to 180°C (350°F) mark 4. To make the date filling, put the water and sugar in a saucepan over a low heat until the sugar is dissolved. Bring to the boil, add the dates and simmer gently, stirring constantly, for 4-5 minutes. Remove from the heat, stir in the lemon juice and allow to cool.

To prepare the rolled oats mixture, cream the butter in a mixing bowl until soft. Add the sugar and beat thoroughly until well creamed. Sift the flour and salt into the bowl and stir well until evenly blended. Dissolve the bicarbonate of soda in the water, then add to the flour mixture, stirring well. Stir in the rolled oats.

Lightly press half of the rolled oats mixture into the bottom of a greased shallow 23 cm (9 inch) square tin. Cover with the cooled date filling, then top with the remaining oat mixture. Press down well. Bake in the preheated oven for about 45 minutes, until golden brown. Cool in the tin, then cut into 4 cm (1½ inch) squares.

CANADIAN EMBASSY

Date and Cherry Teabread

Makes about 10 slices

225 g (8 oz) self-raising flour
pinch of salt
2.5 ml (½ tsp) ground mixed spice
125 g (4 oz) margarine
75 g (3 oz) sugar
125 g (4 oz) cooking dates, chopped
50 g (2 oz) glacé cherries, chopped
1 egg
60 ml (4 tbsp) milk

Preheat the oven to 180°C (350°F) mark 4. Sift the flour with the salt and spice into a mixing bowl. Rub in the margarine until the mixture resembles fine breadcrumbs. Stir in the sugar, chopped dates and cherries.

Beat the egg with the milk, then stir into the cake mixture. Transfer to a greased 1.3 litre (2¼ pint) loaf tin.

Bake in the preheated oven for 1¼ hours until well risen and just firm to the touch. Turn out and cool on a wire rack.

MRS J. WILKS

Moist Lemon Cake

Makes one 20 cm (8 inch) round cake

Make sure you pour the lemon syrup over the cake while it is still warm or it will not be absorbed.

125 g (4 oz) margarine
175 g (6 oz) sugar
finely grated rind of 1 lemon
2 eggs
225 g (8 oz) plain flour
7.5 ml (1½ tsp) baking powder
2.5 ml (½ tsp) salt
120 ml (8 tbsp) milk

FOR THE SYRUP:
juice of 1 lemon
75 g (3 oz) sugar

Preheat the oven to 180°C (350°F) mark 4. Grease and line a 20 cm (8 inch) round cake tin. Cream the margarine and sugar together in a mixing bowl until light and fluffy. Add the lemon rind, then beat in the eggs, one at a time. Sift the flour with the baking powder and salt, then fold into the mixture with the milk.

Turn the mixture into the prepared tin and bake in the preheated oven for 50 minutes to 1 hour until well risen and firm to the touch.

To make the lemon syrup, put the lemon juice and sugar in a small saucepan and heat gently to dissolve.

Turn the cake out on to a wire rack and prick the surface with a fine skewer. Pour the lemon syrup over the cake, then leave until cold.

MRS K. CRAIG

Chocolate Cake with Coffee Cream

Makes one 18 cm (7 inch) round cake

This chocolate cake is delectable with its coffee buttercream filling.

125 g (4 oz) caster sugar
125 g (4 oz) soft vegetable margarine
2 eggs
5 ml (1 tsp) vanilla flavouring
125 g (4 oz) self-raising flour
2.5 ml (½ tsp) baking powder
15 g (½ oz) cocoa powder
15 ml (1 tbsp) milk
5 ml (1 tsp) strong instant coffee granules

FOR THE FILLING:
125 g (4 oz) icing sugar
50 g (2 oz) unsalted butter
5 ml (1 tsp) strong instant coffee granules

FOR THE DECORATION:
50 g (2 oz) plain chocolate

Preheat the oven to 160°C (325°F) mark 3. Grease two 18 cm (7 inch) sandwich tins and line each with a circle of greased greaseproof paper. Put the sugar, margarine, eggs and vanilla into a large bowl or food processor, then sift in the flour, baking powder and cocoa. Beat or process until smooth and slightly glossy, then add the milk and coffee dissolved in 15 ml (1 tbsp) hot water, and beat again, briefly, to blend.

Turn the mixture into the prepared tins and spread evenly. Bake in the preheated oven for 20-25 minutes, or until the centres of the cakes spring back when touched lightly. Leave the cakes in the tins for 5 minutes, then turn out on to a wire rack to cool.

To make the filling, beat the icing sugar and butter together until creamy and light. Dissolve the coffee in 15-30 ml (1-2 tbsp) hot water and beat into the mixture. Sandwich the cakes together with half the coffee cream and spread the rest on top. Decorate with some flakes of plain chocolate, made by drawing a potato peeler down the bar of chocolate whilst holding the chocolate over the top of the cake.

Never-Fail
Boiled Fruit Cake

Makes one 20 cm (8 inch) round cake

This recipe never seems to fail even when I vary the ingredients; it also freezes well. You can use any combination of dried and glacé fruit – such as sultanas, currants and raisins, glacé cherries and crystallized pineapple – including some chopped nuts if you like. You could also replace a little of the liquid with sherry.

350 g (12 oz) mixed dried fruit
250 ml (8 fl oz) mixed fruit juice and water
125 g (4 oz) butter or margarine
125 g (4 oz) brown sugar
5 ml (1 tsp) ground mixed spice
125 g (4 oz) self-raising wholemeal flour
125 g (4 oz) plain wholemeal flour
5 ml (1 tsp) bicarbonate of soda
2 eggs, beaten

Put the dried fruit in a saucepan with the liquid, butter or margarine, sugar and mixed spice. Slowly bring to the boil, then simmer gently for 2 minutes. Remove from the heat and leave to cool for about 1 hour.

Preheat the oven to 180°C (350°F) mark 4. Grease and line a 20 cm (8 inch) round cake tin. Put the flours and bicarbonate of soda into a mixing bowl. Add the fruit mixture with the eggs and mix thoroughly until evenly blended. Pour into the prepared cake tin – the mixture will be quite sloppy.

Bake in the preheated oven for 15 minutes, then lower the temperature to 160°C (325°F) mark 3. Bake for a further 1 hour or until a skewer inserted in the centre comes out clean. Turn out and cool on a wire rack.

MARY RONALDSON • OXFORD

Spiced Raisin Cake with Cashew Nut Topping

Makes one 20 cm (8 inch) square cake

A simple and delicious spiced cake to enjoy at teatime – or anytime with a cup of tea or coffee,

225 g (8 oz) plain flour
3.75 ml (¾ tsp) baking powder
3.75 ml (¾ tsp) bicarbonate of soda
2.5 ml (½ tsp) salt
2.5 ml (½ tsp) freshly grated nutmeg
5 ml (1 tsp) ground cinnamon
150 g (5 oz) caster sugar
125 ml (4 fl oz) vegetable oil
1 egg, beaten
125 ml (4 fl oz) natural yogurt
125 ml (4 fl oz) golden syrup
125 g (4 oz) raisins

FOR THE TOPPING:
50 g (2 oz) granulated sugar
40 g (1½ oz) unsalted cashew nuts, chopped
15 ml (1 tbsp) ground cinnamon

Preheat the oven to 180°C (350°F) mark 4. Sift together the flour, baking powder, bicarbonate of soda, salt and spices. Stir in the sugar and make a well in the centre.

In another bowl, beat the oil with the egg, yogurt and syrup until well blended. Pour into the well in the flour mixture and stir into the flour with the raisins until evenly mixed. Turn the mixture into a greased and lined 20 cm (8 inch) square cake tin.

Mix together the ingredients for the topping and sprinkle evenly over the cake mixture. Bake in the preheated oven for 35-45 minutes. Leave in the tin for 5 minutes, then remove and cool on a wire rack.

Christmas Carrot Cake

Makes one 20 cm (8 inch) round cake

175 g (6 oz) sultanas
60 ml (4 tbsp) whisky
250 ml (8 fl oz) corn oil
100 g (4 oz) molasses sugar
3 eggs, size 1
15 ml (1 tbsp) cocoa powder
225 g (8 oz) plain wholemeal flour
5 ml (1 tsp) ground cinnamon
2.5 ml (½ tsp) freshly grated nutmeg
2.5 ml (½ tsp) ground allspice
2.5 ml (½ tsp) salt
7.5 ml (1½ tsp) baking powder
7.5 ml (1½ tsp) bicarbonate of soda
225 g (8 oz) carrots, finely grated
75 g (3 oz) walnuts, finely chopped

FOR THE ICING:
50 g (2 oz) icing sugar
350 g (12 oz) low-fat soft cheese
finely grated rind of ½ lemon

Put the sultanas in a small bowl, pour on the whisky, stir and leave to soak for 1 hour or longer.

Preheat the oven to 180°C (350°F) mark 4. Line a loose-bottomed 20 cm (8 inch) round cake tin with non-stick baking parchment, or greased and floured greaseproof paper. In a large mixing bowl, beat together the oil and sugar, then beat in the eggs one at a time. (At this stage the mixture looks very odd, but don't worry!) Still beating, add the cocoa, flour, spices, salt, baking powder and bicarbonate of soda. Add the carrots, sultanas and whisky, with the nuts and stir until evenly mixed.

Turn the mixture into the prepared tin. Bake in the preheated oven for about 1¼ hours, until a warmed skewer inserted into the centre of the cake comes out clean. Leave the cake in the tin to cool.

To make the icing, work the icing sugar into the soft cheese with the lemon rind until evenly blended. Spread the icing over the cake when it is quite cold.

JOAN HENRY • GLENROTHES, FIFE

Quick Celebration Cake

Makes one large ring cake

A quick and easy ring cake, which can be decorated to suit any occasion. For a festive touch finish with a few holly sprigs.

125 g (4 oz) concentrated butter
125 g (4 oz) soft light brown sugar
2 eggs, size 3, beaten
225 g (8 oz) self-raising flour
pinch of salt
5 ml (1 tsp) ground mixed spice
225 g (8 oz) can pineapple rings, drained and chopped
25 g (1 oz) walnuts, chopped
25 g (1 oz) desiccated coconut
125 g (4 oz) sultanas
75 g (3 oz) mixed peel, chopped
75 g (3 oz) glacé cherries, rinsed and halved

FOR THE ICING:
40 g (1½ oz) concentrated butter
175 g (6 oz) icing sugar
15 ml (1 tbsp) pineapple juice
25 g (1 oz) desiccated coconut

TO DECORATE:
glacé fruits, eg pineapple and cherries or toasted flaked coconut (optional)

Preheat the oven to 150°C (300°F) mark 2. In a mixing bowl, cream the butter until soft and smooth, then add the sugar and beat until light and fluffy. Gradually beat in the eggs. Sift together the flour, salt and mixed spice, then fold into the creamed mixture with the chopped pineapple, nuts, coconut, sultanas, chopped peel and cherries.

Spoon the mixture into a greased 1.2 litre (2½ pint) ring mould. Bake in the preheated oven for 1¼ hours. Leave to cool in the tin.

For the icing, beat the butter until soft and smooth, then add the icing sugar, pineapple juice and coconut. Beat thoroughly until evenly blended. Turn the cake out of the tin and roughly spread the icing over the top. Decorate with glacé fruits or toasted coconut, or as desired.

JUDY BUGG

Preserves and Drinks

Three Fruit Marmalade

Makes about 4.5 kg (10 lb)

This is an easy marmalade recipe, made all the easier if you have a sugar thermometer, which takes all the guesswork out of discovering when setting point has been reached. I do recommend that you use a preserving pan for making this quantity; alternatively halve the ingredients and use your largest saucepan. To sterilize jars, first wash thoroughly, then dry off in a cool oven at 140°C (275°F) mark 1 for about 30 minutes. Fill while still warm.

1 grapefruit
4 sweet oranges
2 lemons
2.7 kg (6 lb) sugar
knob of butter or margarine

Wash the fruit, and cut the grapefruit into quarters. Put the fruit into a large saucepan, or into a pressure cooker. Add 1.7 litres (3 pints) water (only 900 ml/1½ pints if you're using a pressure cooker). Boil, or cook under pressure, until the fruit is very soft: about 1 hour 15 minutes in a saucepan; 25 minutes in a pressure cooker.

Leave to cool, then strain off and reserve the liquid. Scoop the pulp out of the skins and press through a sieve, discarding the pips and pith residue. Cut the skins into thin pieces and add to the reserved liquid with the sieved pulp.

Measure the quantity of fruit and liquid, then put it into a preserving pan and add enough cold water to bring the total quantity up to 3.5 litres (6 pints); you will need to add about 1.2 litres (2 pints) water. Bring to a rolling boil then add the sugar. Boil steadily, stirring from time to time, until setting point is reached, ie 110°C (225°F) as registered on a sugar thermometer, or when a little of the marmalade put onto a cold saucer wrinkles when pushed with a finger. Add the butter or margarine to disperse the scum and leave to cool a little. Pour into hot, sterilised jars, cool, then seal when cold.

ROSE ELLIOT

Marrow and Ginger Jam

Makes about 2 kg (4½ lb)

1 kg (2 lb) mature yellow marrow
salt
1 kg (2 lb) sugar
finely pared rind and juice of 1 lemon
125 g (4 oz) crystallized ginger, chopped

Peel the marrow, cut it into small dice and place in a colander. Sprinkle with salt, cover with a plate and put a weight on top. Leave for 12 hours, then rinse and dry well. Put into a bowl with the sugar and leave for another 12 hours.

Transfer the marrow to a preserving pan or large heavy-based pan and add the lemon and ginger. Cook gently over a low heat until the marrow is transparent and a little of the syrup sets when tested on a cold saucer.

Pour into hot sterilized jars, cool, then seal and store in a cool dry place.

ROSE ELLIOT

Marrow Chutney

Makes about 1.8 kg (4 lb)

1.5 kg (3 lb) marrow
450 g (1 lb) onions, sliced
450 g (1 lb) cooking apples
450 g (1 lb) cooking dates, roughly chopped
600 ml (1 pint) malt vinegar
1 kg (2 lb) sugar
5 ml (1 tsp) salt
5 ml (1 tsp) ground ginger
45 ml (3 tbsp) pickling spices

Peel and dice the marrow and place in a preserving pan or large saucepan with the onions. Peel, quarter, core and slice the apples and add to the pan with the dates. Pour the vinegar into the pan and add the sugar, salt and ginger. Tie the pickling spices in a piece of muslin and immerse in the mixture.

Bring slowly to the boil, then lower the heat and simmer gently until thick and brown. Allow to cool, then remove the bag of pickling spices. Pot into sterilized jars, cover and store in a cool place.

ROSE ELLIOT

Loveday's Spiced Oranges

Makes about 4.5-5 kg (10 lb)

This delicious recipe was given to me one Christmas by my friend, Loveday, together with a jar of the delectable spiced oranges – which go well with many savoury dishes.

12 thin-skinned oranges
1.1 kg (2½ lb) brown sugar
600 ml (1 pint) wine vinegar or cider vinegar
12 whole cloves
10 cm (4 inch) cinnamon stick
6-8 blades of mace or 2.5 ml (½ tsp) ground mace

Wash and dry the oranges, then cut into slices about 5 mm (¼ inch) thick. Remove any pips and put the orange slices into a large pan. Cover with cold water, bring to the boil and simmer gently, covered, for 20-30 minutes, or until the orange skin is just tender.

Meanwhile, in another pan, bring the remaining ingredients slowly to the boil, stirring until the sugar has dissolved. Boil for 3 minutes. Remove the orange slices from their pan with a slotted spoon and add them to the spiced vinegar along with enough of their cooking water to cover them. Simmer the orange slices for 35-40 minutes until they are completely tender, but take care to ensure they do not disintegrate. Remove from the heat and leave the oranges to stand in the syrup for 24 hours.

Using a slotted spoon, carefully remove the orange slices from the syrup and put them into sterilised jars, filling them no more than half full. Bring the syrup to the boil, then boil for a few minutes to reduce. Leave to cool a little, then pour into the jars, filling them to the top. Seal. The spiced oranges are ready to eat after about one month.

ROSE ELLIOT

Almond
and Strawberry Shake

Serves 1

This is a healthy and nutritious drink, with a delicious flavour. It makes a filling snack or light meal.

50 g (2 oz) shelled almonds
50 g (2 oz) fresh or frozen strawberries
2.5 cm (1 inch) piece vanilla pod, or few drops of real vanilla essence
150 ml (¼ pint) water
5 ml (1 tsp) honey
strawberry slices to decorate

Skin the almonds by putting them in a small saucepan, covering with water and bringing to the boil. Boil for 1 minute, then remove from the heat, drain the almonds and slip off their skins. Put the almonds into a blender or food processor. Hull the strawberries if you're using fresh ones, then put the strawberries into the blender with the vanilla pod or essence and a little of the water. Whizz to a creamy purée, then add the rest of the water with the honey, and whizz again.

Pour the drink into a glass and serve at once, decorated with some strawberry slices. Alternatively the mixture can be poured through a sieve into the glass if you want a very smooth drink, and it can be diluted with a little more water if you want a thinner consistency.

ROSE ELLIOT

Mango Smoothie

Serves 1

A sweet and refreshing drink – perfect for a hot summer's day.

1 medium mango
water to mix

Halve the mango and remove the stone at the same time, by making two downward cuts, each about 5 mm (¼ inch) from the stalk. Peel the mango and cut the flesh away from the stone. Put the mango flesh into a blender or food processor with a little water and whizz until smooth, then add more water, to bring the mixture to the desired consistency.

ROSE ELLIOT

Sangria

Serves 3-4

This popular Mexican drink is deliciously refreshing.

225 g (8 oz) sugar
250 ml (8 fl oz) water
600 ml (1 pint) orange juice
250 ml (8 fl oz) red wine
30 ml (2 tbsp) lemon juice
chopped apples or peaches (optional)
crushed ice to serve

Put the sugar and water into a small saucepan and heat gently until the sugar is dissolved. Leave to cool.

Mix the orange juice with the sugar syrup, red wine and lemon juice. If desired, add chopped apples or peaches. Serve in tall glasses with crushed ice.

Festive Fruit Punch

Serves 10

In Guatemala this unique hot punch is reserved for special occasions such as weddings, Christmas or the New Year, when the climate is cool. It is worth experimenting with different fruit combinations.

1 medium pineapple
1 papaya
5 apples
175 g (6 oz) prunes or raisins
1 bunch seedless grapes
2 litres (3½ pints) water
125 g (4 oz) sugar
4 cinnamon sticks
4 cloves
pinch of salt (optional)
rum to taste (optional)

First prepare the fruit. Peel, halve and core the pineapple, then chop finely or purée in a blender or food processor. Peel the papaya, halve and remove the seeds. Peel, quarter, core and chop the apples. Stone and chop the prunes if using.

Bring the water to the boil in a large saucepan. Add the pineapple, papaya, apples, prunes or raisins and grapes. Stir in the sugar, spices and salt if using. Simmer gently until the fruit is soft.

Just before serving, add rum to taste if desired. Serve hot, providing spoons for everyone to eat the fruit.

Lassi

Serves 10

*This cold mint beverage is a variation of a popular South Asian drink.
Similar drinks are served in parts of the Middle East. Lassi is a lovely refreshing
accompaniment to hot spicy foods. The proportions of the ingredients can
be varied according to taste.*

**1 litre (1¾ pints) milk
1 litre (1¾ pints) natural yogurt
125-175 g (4-6 oz) sugar, or a mixture of sugar and honey
20 ml (4 tsp) vanilla flavouring
6-8 mint sprigs**

In a large jug or bowl mix together the milk, yogurt, sugar and vanilla flavouring.
Stir well.

Bruise the mint leaves to release their flavour and tie the ends of the stalks
together with string. Immerse the mint in the drink.

Cover and let stand in the refrigerator for at least 5 hours before serving to
allow the flavour of the mint to permeate the drink. Remove the mint sprigs
before serving.

Louis Tea

Serves 1

*This recipe was given to me by Louis Satterfield, hence the name. I find it's good
for my throat so I drink it in the studio, on tour, etc.*

large pinch of peppermint tea
large pinch of comfrey tea
small pinch of gold seal tea
boiling water to infuse
juice of ½ lemon
10 ml (2 tsp) honey, or to taste
liberal pinch of cayenne pepper

Take a large pinch of loose peppermint tea, a large pinch of comfrey tea and a
small pinch of gold seal tea. Place all in a teapot and add boiling water.
Meanwhile, squeeze the juice of ½ lemon into a flask and add approximately
2 teaspoons of honey, or to taste really. Add a liberal pinch of cayenne pepper –
I use a lot! When the tea is brewed – allow normal time – pour into the flask,
shake well and drink.

PHIL COLLINS

Index

A

almonds: almond and
celery soup, 22
almond and strawberry
shake, 181
apple almond, 144
Manomin pancakes, 140
millet with spring
onions and almonds,
75
mixed rice salad with
nuts and apricots, 81
nut pâté, 132
peach and almond
tranche, 146-7
apples: apple and fennel
salad, 48
apple almond, 144
marrow chutney, 179
pommes au beurre, 147
yummy yams, 149
apricots: rice salad with
nuts and apricots, 81
artichokes: mixed rice
with artichoke hearts,
74
roasted pepper,
aubergine and
artichoke salad, 45
artichokes, Jerusalem *see*
Jerusalem artichokes
asparagus: asparagus and
goat's cheese strudel,
97
asparagus salad, 43
asparagus soup, 16
aubergines: aubergine and
yogurt relish, 57
aubergines in coconut,
55
green peppers with
aubergine stuffing,
122
penne with onion,
peppers and
aubergine, 62

Provençal bean
casserole, 86
roasted pepper,
aubergine and
artichoke salad, 45
Aunt Bella's nutmeat,
131
avocados: celery and
avocado salad, 47
tomatoes with
guacamole, 28
Victoria Wood's best
sandwich ever, 36

B

baked bananas, 153
baked beans, homemade,
91
baked corn, 83
baked orange pears with
spiced cream, 148
bananas: baked bananas,
153
banana and cashew nut
curry, 135
carrot and banana
salad, 40
sweet potato casserole,
55
basil: spaghetti with
homemade pesto, 63
beans *see also* individual
types of bean
beans Granados, 88
sprouting, 38
beetroot julienne with
caraway, 50
Beverley Hills
cheesecake, 151
biscuits: cheese biscuits,
163
Irish shortbread, 164
black beans: hot black
bean and rice salad
with pomegranates,
84

black-eyed beans:
creamed beans and
sweet potatoes, 88
homemade baked
beans, 91
bobotie: nut bobotie with
Cape rice, 138-9
brazil nuts: cheesy nut
rissoles, 137
bread: cheese and celery
loaf, 162
easy homemade bread,
160
Healy's cottage bread,
161
broad bean cutlets with
onion sauce, 125
broccoli: broccoli
supreme, 112
pasta with broccoli, 68
Brussels chicory, 52
burgers: vegi-burgers, 133
butter beans: creamy
potato, parsnip and
butter bean soup, 20

C

cabbage: cabbage in
tomato sauce, 54
cabbage with garlic
butter, 51
stuffed cabbage rolls,
120
cakes: chocolate cake
with coffee cream, 172
Christmas carrot cake,
175
moist lemon cake, 171
never fail boiled fruit
cake, 173
quick celebration cake,
176
spiced raisin cake with
cashew topping, 174
cannellini beans with red
peppers and olives, 87

cannelloni, vegetarian, 69
Cape rice, nut bobotie
   with, 138-9
caraway, beetroot julienne
   with, 50
carnival macaroni cheese,
   71
carrots: carrot and banana
   salad, 40
   carrot and parsnip
      julienne, 53
   Christmas carrot cake,
      175
   Middle Eastern carrot
      salad, 39
   pine nut and carrot
      roast with mushroom
      sauce, 128
cashew nuts: banana and
   cashew nut curry, 135
   cheesy nut rissoles, 137
   pea and cashew nut
      stew, 136
   spiced raisin cake with
      cashew nut topping,
      174
casseroles: Mexican
   pepper casserole, 118
   pea and cashew nut
      stew, 136
   Provençal bean
      casserole, 86
   sweet potato casserole,
      55
   vegetable and lentil
      casserole, 119
cauliflower bake,
   cheesy, 115
celery: almond and celery
   soup, 22
   celery and avocado
      salad, 47
   celery and mushroom
      pasta, 65
   cheese and celery loaf,
      162
champ, 60
channa dal, 92
cheese: asparagus and
   goat's cheese strudel,
   97
   baked corn, 83

baked feta cheese and
   spinach omelette, 114
carnival macaroni
   cheese, 71
carrot and banana salad,
   40
cheese and celery loaf,
   162
cheese and lentil loaf,
   94
cheese and onion flan,
   99
cheese and potato balls,
   35
cheese biscuits, 163
cheese croûtons, 23
cheese ramekins, 35
cheesy cauliflower bake,
   115
cheesy nut rissoles, 137
courgette and cheese
   bake, 110
Greek spinach pie, 106
lasagne, 70-1
Mexican pepper
   casserole, 118
mixed salad with
   Parmesan cheese, 41
mushroom roulade, 116
pancakes with tomato
   and walnut stuffing,
   130-1
pear and cream cheese
   salad, 44
potatoes with creamy
   tomato sauce, 124
spaghetti with
   homemade pesto, 63
stuffed cabbage rolls,
   120
that veggy quiche
   without pastry, 113
vegetarian cannelloni,
   69
cheesecakes: Beverley
   Hills, 151
glazed saffron
   cheesecakes, 152-3
cherries: date and cherry
   teabread, 170
chestnut stuffing, red
   peppers with, 121

chick peas: channa dal, 92
   chick pea and spinach
      pâté, 30
chicory, Brussels, 52
chilli, Kirsty's, 90
chocolate: chocolate cake
   with coffee cream, 172
   chocolate macaroon
      fingers, 166
   chocolate mousse, 154
   chocolate pots with
      mint cream, 155
   red fruit compote with
      chocolate terrine, 142
Christmas carrot cake,
   175
chutney, marrow, 179
coconut: aubergines in
   coconut, 55
   chocolate macaroon
      fingers, 166
   nutty slack, 168
coffee cream, chocolate
   cake with, 172
corn see sweetcorn
courgettes: courgette and
   cheese bake, 110
   courgette and tomato
      gratin, 109
   Provençal bean
      casserole, 86
cream: mint, 155
   spiced, 148
creamed beans and sweet
   potatoes, 88
croûtons, cheese, 23
crumbles: fruit, 145
   root vegetable, 117
curries: banana and
   cashew nut curry, 135
   curried wild rice salad,
      42

D

dates: date and cherry
   teabread, 170
   date squares, 169
   marrow chutney, 179
   nutty slack, 168
   treacle and date scones,
      165
desserts, 141-58

drinks, 181-5
  almond and strawberry shake, 181
  festive fruit punch, 183
  lassi, 184
  Louis tea, 185
  mango smoothie, 182
  sangria, 182

E
easy homemade bread, 160
eggs: baked feta cheese and spinach omelette, 114

F
fennel: apple and fennel salad, 48
festive fruit punch, 183
flageolet beans: Provençal bean casserole, 86
flans and quiches: cheese and onion flan, 99
  leek and mustard quiche, 101
  onion flan 98
  righteous lentil flan, 102
  spinach quiche, 100
  sweetcorn soufflé flan, 99
  that veggy quiche without pastry, 113
fragrant saffron pilau, 79
fritters, sweetcorn, 82
fruit see also individual types of fruit
  festive fruit punch, 183
  fruit crumble, 145
  pavlova, 156
  red fruit compote with chocolate terrine, 142
fruit cakes: never fail boiled fruit cake, 173
  spiced raisin cake with cashew nut topping, 174

G
garlic butter, cabbage with, 51

ginger: Lancashire parkin, 167
  marrow and ginger jam, 179
glazed saffron cheesecakes, 152-3
goat's cheese: asparagus and goat's cheese strudel, 97
grain and rice dishes, 73-84
grapefruit: three fruit marmalade, 178
gratin, courgette and tomato, 109
Greek spinach pie, 106
green beans with cumin, 56
guacamole, tomatoes with, 28

H
haricot bean salad, 89
hazelnuts: hazelnut torte, 150
  mixed nut roast, 129
Healy's cottage bread, 161
herb soup, iced, 26
homemade baked beans, 91
honey: raspberry and honey ice cream, 158

I
ice cream: raspberry and honey, 158
  rum, 157
Irish shortbread, 164

J
jam, marrow and ginger 179
Jerusalem artichokes: nutty artichokes, 139

K
Kingsmead leek and potato puffs, 103
Kirsty's chilli, 90

L
Lancashire parkin, 167

lasagne, 70-1
lassi, 184
leeks: Kingsmead leek and potato puffs, 103
  leek and mustard quiche, 101
  that veggy quiche without pastry, 113
  vegetable and noodle crunch, 67
  vichyssoise soup, 24
lemon: moist lemon cake, 171
  three fruit marmalade, 178
lentils: cheese and lentil loaf, 94
  lentil and tomato soup, 17
  righteous lentil flan, 102
  spinach dal, 93
  Turkish lentil soup, 21
  vegetable and lentil casserole, 119
Louis tea, 185
Loveday's spiced oranges, 180

M
macaroni: carnival macaroni cheese, 71
  vegetable macaroni bake, 64
macaroon fingers, chocolate, 166
mango smoothie, 182
Manomin pancakes, 140
marmalade, three fruit, 178
marrow: marrow and ginger jam, 179
  marrow chutney, 179
  marrow rice, 76
  marrow with crispy stuffing, 123
meringue, pavlova, 156
Mexican pepper casserole, 118
Middle Eastern carrot salad, 39
midweek soup, 18

milk: lassi, 184
millet with spring onions and almonds, 75
mint: chocolate pots with mint cream, 155
lassi, 184
mixed nut roast, 129
moist lemon cake, 171
moong dal: spinach dal, 93
mousse, chocolate, 154
mushrooms: celery and mushroom pasta, 65
fragrant saffron pilau, 79
marrow with crispy stuffing, 123
mushroom pâté, 29
mushroom roulade, 116
mushroom stroganoff, 126
oyster mushroom and pine nut tartlets, 96
pine nut and carrot roast with mushroom sauce, 128
Provençal bean casserole, 86
risotto Piedmontaise, 77
stuffed mushrooms, 32
Swiss mushrooms, 33
mustard: leek and mustard quiche, 101

N

nectarines: glazed saffron cheesecakes, 152-3
never fail boiled fruit cake, 173
noodles: vegetable and noodle crunch, 67
nuts, 127-40 see also individual types of nut
Aunt Bella's nutmeat, 131
marrow with crispy stuffing, 123
mixed nut roast, 129
nut bobotie with Cape rice, 138-9
nut pâté, 132
nutty artichokes, 139

nutty slack, 168
vegi-burgers, 133

O

oats: date squares, 169
Lancashire parkin, 167
nutty slack, 168
olives: cannellini beans with red peppers and olives, 87
omelette, baked feta cheese and spinach, 114
onions: broad bean cutlets with onion sauce, 125
cheese and onion flan, 99
marrow chutney, 179
onion flan, 98
penne with onion, peppers and aubergine, 62
orange: baked orange pears with spiced cream, 148
Loveday's spiced oranges, 180
three fruit marmalade, 178
orange juice: sangria, 182
oyster mushroom and pine nut tartlets, 96

P

pakoras, 34
pancakes: Manomin pancakes, 140
pancakes with tomato and walnut stuffing, 130-1
pumpkin pancakes, 33
parkin, Lancashire, 167
parsnips: carrot and parsnip julienne, 53
creamy potato, parsnip and butter bean soup, 20
pasta dishes, 61-72
pasta shapes: pasta with broccoli, 68
pasta shells: celery and mushroom pasta, 65

vegetable pastition, 66
pastries, glazed vegetable, 31
pastry dishes, savoury, 95-106
pâtés: chick pea and spinach, 30
mushroom, 29
nut, 132
pavlova, 156
peaches: peach and almond tranche, 146-7
peaches in spiced wine, 143
peanuts: peanut and potato rissoles, 134
peanut soup, 19
pears: baked orange pears with spiced cream, 148
pear and cream cheese salad, 44
peas: pea and cashew nut stew, 136
risotto Piedmontaise, 77
penne: penne with onion, peppers and aubergine, 62
pink pasta, 72
peppermint: chocolate pots with mint cream, 155
peppers: cannellini beans with red peppers and olives, 87
green peppers with aubergine stuffing, 122
Kirsty's chilli, 90
Mexican pepper casserole, 118
penne with onion, peppers and aubergine, 62
red peppers with chestnut stuffing, 121
rice with sweet pepper relish, 78
roasted pepper, aubergine and artichoke salad, 45
that veggy quiche without pastry, 113

pesto: spaghetti with homemade pesto, 63

pilaf, spinach and wild rice, 80

pilau, fragrant saffron, 79

pine nuts: oyster mushroom and pine nut tartlets, 96

pine nut and carrot roast with mushroom sauce, 128

spaghetti with homemade pesto, 63

pineapple: quick celebration cake, 176

pink pasta, 72

pomegranates, hot black bean and rice salad with, 84

pommes au beurre, 147

potatoes: champ, 60

cheese and potato balls, 35

creamy potato, parsnip and butter bean soup, 20

Kingsmead leek and potato puffs, 103

peanut and potato rissoles, 134

potatoes with creamy tomato sauce, 124

vichyssoise soup, 24

potatoes, sweet *see* sweet potatoes

preserves, 177-80

Provençal bean casserole, 86

puddings, 141-58

pumpkin: pumpkin pancakes, 33

pumpkin soup with cheese croûtons, 23

punch, festive fruit, 183

Q

quiches *see* flans and quiches

quick celebration cake, 176

R

raisins: spiced raisin cake with cashew nut topping, 174

raspberry and honey ice cream, 158

red fruit compote with chocolate terrine, 142

red kidney beans: beans Granados, 88

Kirsty's chilli, 90

relishes: aubergine and yogurt, 57

sweet pepper, 78

rice: *see also* wild rice

fragrant saffron pilau, 79

hot black bean and rice salad with pomegranates, 84

marrow rice, 76

mixed rice salad with nuts and apricots, 81

mixed rice with artichoke hearts, 74

nut bobotie with Cape rice, 138-9

rice with sweet pepper relish, 78

risotto Piedmontaise, 77

righteous lentil flan, 102

risotto Piedmontaise, 77

rissoles: cheesy nut, 137

peanut and potato, 134

root vegetable crumble, 117

roulade, mushroom, 116

rum ice cream, 157

S

saffron: fragrant saffron pilau, 79

glazed saffron cheesecakes, 152-3

salads, 37-48

apple and fennel, 48

asparagus, 43

carrot and banana, 40

celery and avocado, 47

curried wild rice, 42

haricot bean, 89

hot black bean and rice salad with pomegranates, 84

Middle Eastern carrot, 39

mixed rice salad with nuts and apricots, 81

mixed salad with Parmesan cheese, 41

pear and cream cheese, 44

roasted pepper, aubergine and artichoke, 45

village salad, 46

vitality salad lunch, 38

samosas, vegetable, 104

sandwiches: Victoria Wood's best sandwich ever, 36

sangria, 182

sauces: creamy tomato, 124

green tomato, 58

mushroom, 128

onion, 125

tomato, 54

savoury pastry dishes, 95-106

scones, treacle and date, 165

seeds: sprouting, 38

vegi-burgers, 133

shortbread, Irish, 164

snacks, 27-36

soups, 15-26

almond and celery, 22

asparagus, 16

creamy potato, parsnip and butter bean, 20

fresh corn, 25

iced herb, 26

lentil and tomato, 17

midweek soup, 18

peanut, 19

pumpkin soup with cheese croûtons, 23

Turkish lentil, 21

vichyssoise, 24

spaghetti with homemade pesto, 63

spanokopita, 106

spiced cream, 148
spiced raisin cake with
    cashew nut topping,
    174
spinach: baked feta
    cheese and spinach
    omelette, 114
    chick pea and spinach
    pâté, 30
    Greek spinach pie, 106
    spinach and wild rice
    pilaf, 80
    spinach dal, 93
    spinach quiche, 100
    vegetarian cannelloni,
    69
spring onions: champ, 60
    millet with spring
    onions and almonds,
    75
spring rolls, 105
sprouting beans, 38
squash: beans Granados,
    88
starters, 27-36
stews see casseroles
strawberries: almond and
    strawberry shake, 181
strudel, asparagus and
    goat's cheese, 97
sultanas: Christmas carrot
    cake, 175
super stir-fry, 108
sweet potatoes: creamed
    beans and sweet
    potatoes 88
    sweet potato casserole,
    55
sweetcorn: baked corn, 83
    beans Granados, 88
    fresh corn soup, 25
    sweetcorn fritters, 82
    sweetcorn soufflé flan,
    99
Swiss mushrooms, 33

T

tartlets, oyster mushroom
    and pine nut, 96
tarts, sweet see also
    cheesecakes
    hazelnut torte, 150

peach and almond
    tranche, 146-7
tea, Louis, 185
teabread, date and cherry,
    170
that veggy quiche without
    pastry, 113
three fruit marmalade,
    178
tomatoes: cabbage in
    tomato sauce, 54
    courgette and cheese
    bake, 110
    courgette and tomato
    gratin, 109
    green beans with cumin,
    56
    green tomato sauce, 58
    homemade baked
    beans, 91
    lasagne, 70-1
    lentil and tomato soup,
    17
    pancakes with tomato
    and walnut stuffing,
    130-1
    potatoes with creamy
    tomato sauce, 124
    Provencal bean
    casserole, 86
    tomatoes with
    guacamole, 28
    vegetarian cannelloni,
    69
    Victoria Wood's best
    sandwich ever, 36
torte, hazelnut, 150
tranche, peach and
    almond, 146-7
treacle and date scones,
    165
Turkish lentil soup, 21

V

vegetables: see also salads
    and individual types
    of vegetable
    accompaniments, 49-60
    assorted vegetable
    sauté, 59
    glazed vegetable
    pastries, 31

main vegetable dishes,
    107-26
pakoras, 34
root vegetable crumble,
    117
super stir-fry, 108
vegetable and lentil
    casserole, 119
vegetable and noodle
    crunch, 67
vegetable macaroni
    bake, 64
vegetable pastition, 66
vegetable samosas, 104
vegetarian winter
    savoury, 111
vegetarian cannelloni, 69
vegetarian winter savoury,
    111
vegi-burgers, 133
vichyssoise soup, 24
Victoria Wood's best
    sandwich ever, 36
village salad, 46
vitality salad lunch, 38

W

walnuts: mixed nut roast,
    129
    nutty artichokes, 139
    pancakes with tomato
    and walnut stuffing,
    130-1
wild rice: curried wild rice
    salad, 42
    Manomin pancakes, 140
    mixed rice salad with
    nuts and apricots, 81
    spinach and wild rice
    pilaf, 80
wine: peaches in spiced
    wine, 143
    sangria, 182

Y

yams, yummy, 149
yogurt: aubergine and
    yogurt relish, 57
    lassi, 184
    raspberry and honey ice
    cream, 158
yummy yams, 149

Acknowledgements

Oxfam, Rose Elliot and the Publishers would like to thank Oxfam's supporters, volunteers and staff for contributing so actively to this collection, and the following for permission to use recipes from their publications:

Bridgehead Inc., the trading arm of Oxfam Canada, for recipes on pages 42, 53, 80, 137, 140, 149, 172 and 174 which first appeared in *A Taste for Justice,* now out of print; Community Aid Abroad Australia for recipes on pages 43, 47, 82, 88 (both), 105, 122 and 182 which first appeared in *The CAA Vegetarian Cook Book;* Herald Press and their contributors for the recipes on pages 54, 59, 70-1, 106, 124, 183 and 184 which first appeared in *Extending the Table,* published by Herald Press, Scottdale, Pennsylvania.

The recipes on pages 25, 34, 41, 46, 83, 89, 92, 134, 136 and 153 are based on material from *Recipes from Around the World,* published by Oxfam in 1983. Those on pages 25 and 153 first appeared in *CIIR Overseas Volunteers News* and are reproduced with permission of the Catholic Institution for International Relations; on pages 34, 92 and 136 in *Cooking the Indian Way* by Attia Hosain and Sita Pasricha, published by Hamlyn Publishing Group; on page 89 in *A Book of Middle Eastern Food* by Claudia Roden, published by Penguin Books: all reproduced by permission.

Finally, thanks are due to all those who have given their recipes to Oxfam over the years. The first national 'Oxfam Recipe Book' was *Chefs Galore,* devised in Northern Ireland and published in 1962. It is such a rich source of tried and tested recipes and interesting celebrity contributions that we have used a number of recipes from it – adapted where necessary for a current readership: these appear on pages 22, 24, 32, 33, 35 (both), 44, 52, 71, 99, 104, 147, 148, 151, 154, 156, 157, 158, 163, 164, 166, 169, 170 and 171.